THROUGH THE LICH-GATE

A BIOGRAPHY OF THE LITTLE CHURCH AROUND THE CORNER

Imp R L B   R L Boyer

THROUGH THE LICH GATE

THROUGH THE LICH-GATE

A BIOGRAPHY OF
THE LITTLE CHURCH AROUND THE CORNER

BY ISHBEL ROSS

Sixteen Illustrations from Dry Points by
RALPH L. BOYER

NEW YORK
WILLIAM FARQUHAR PAYSON
1931

Copyright, 1931

WILLIAM FARQUHAR PAYSON
INCORPORATED

NEW YORK

Printed and Bound in the
UNITED STATES OF AMERICA

TABLE OF CONTENTS

LIST OF ILLUSTRATIONS

I

QUIET ACRE

THE Little Church Around the Corner, which first opened its doors
on country lanes in 1850, nestles in verdant seclusion to-day among steel-
ribbed acres of peaks and spires, as full of peace as it was when commerce
lay far south of its sheltering *close*. It stands on the same site as it did in old
New York, a jewel in an antique setting worn by an ultra-modern woman.
One step off Fifth Avenue, it drowses under the last of its tall English elms.
Between the church and the street the lich-gate spreads its shade, inviting
passersby to pause awhile under its mediæval roof.

On June days, when romance walks enchanted down its soft-hued aisles,
the sunshine stipples the gabled roof and filters through stained glass to
spread a carpet of tinted beams along the path of the brides. In winter the
ice-encrusted towers keep calm vigil among their tall, proud neighbours, a
link with the days when horse-car bells tinkled through frosty air and lamp-
lit rooms encompassed the family life. The spiked iron fence surrounding the
church for three-quarters of a century has stood as a symbol between the
dissonant forces of a growing city and the serenity within. A history of tolerance and charity, a long cycle of birth, death and marriage, have created
their own tradition around the puce-coloured stones of the rambling edifice
entered on the diocesan records as the Church of the Transfiguration but
more widely known by the title Joe Jefferson gave it in 1870. Neither controversy nor ecclesiastical dissension has lit on the vine-clad eaves, and its
accolade of happiness has followed its brides beyond the seven seas, drawing
their children back again in quest of the same beneficent ministration.

To-day The Little Church Around the Corner holds the world's record for marriages and divides its fame between its brides and its stage following.

On a March day in the middle of the last century, Dr. George Hendric Houghton, founder of the parish, opened a plain pine door for services in a rural and sequestered New York. The trees and grass that surrounded the small building were part of the landscape, for the new Episcopal church was dashingly far uptown, society still lounging in the neighbourhood of Washington Square and farther south. The first bride was a seventeen-year-old girl weighing ninety pounds and slim for her generation. Her chestnut brown hair, parted in the centre, swept straight down from her forehead over her ears, and her large grey eyes looked out on the simplest of altars. She wore a dress of fine white mull, and the wide skirt, billowing out from her eighteen-inch waist, was looped with orange blossoms. Two clusters of the bridal blossom fastened a Brussels lace veil to her hair. Her name was Serena Margaretta Keeler and the bridegroom was a dry goods merchant, George Chance Eyland.

Little did the demure Serena dream of the endless procession of brides that would follow her down this aisle, so constant a stream that in eighty years the church has become a matrimonial shrine where nearly 100,000 persons have taken their nuptial vows. Each of its three rectors has found romance inseparable from The Little Church Around the Corner, in spite of the barriers of strict canonical observance that prevent at least two hundred couples from being married there each month. For forty-seven years the founder gave his blessing to the brides of the Victorian era in an interior that evolved from the austerity of a mission house to the glowing beauty of a small cathedral, where old paintings glimmered in dusky alcoves and jewelled fragments of light, tinged with gold, streamed from memorial windows over the worshippers in the pews.

It was during the rectorate of the founder's nephew, the Rev. Dr. George Clarke Houghton, that Transfiguration became known far and wide as the marrying church. For twenty-six years he wove the spell of the parish around its bridal couples, although the idyll of his own life ended with the death of his wife during his early days at 1 East Twenty-ninth Street. After him came the Rev. Dr. Randolph Ray, the third rector to carry on the tradition of the church. In the first seven years of his incumbency he married 15,000 couples, and the record for one day was established on June 28, 1930, when forty-three brides carried their wedding bouquets through the lich-gate.

The sentiment surrounding the brides' altar is so established now that those who kneel on the mulberry velvet cushions before it feel that their path must be strewn with the rose leaves of romance. The roar and grime of the city are distant and dim as they stand before the priest in the Chapel of the Holy Family, surrounded by saints in niches and rare old carvings. The tabernacle upon which they gaze is encrusted with diamonds, rubies, emeralds, sapphires—sparkling gems taken from old engagement rings and family heirlooms—the gifts of happy brides of the past. A tradition as elusive as the ghost voices that the superstitious believe can be heard under the tower of St. Joseph's Mortuary Chapel clings to the church where Edwin Booth and O. Henry were buried; where Mr. and Mrs. Stuyvesant Fish were married in the '70's, and Mrs. Astor brought her following; where Negroes were succoured during the Civil War riots, and bread lines were established in time of need; where the stage joined hands with the church many years ago and continued to seek the offices of marriage, baptism and burial at its liberal altar.

In the raftered Guild Hall the amber light from mullioned windows falls athwart the yellowing playbills of long ago, and here the bride may adjust her veil before Kate Claxton's pier mirror or write a note on Richard Mansfield's oak table. Downstairs in the church the record of its long theatrical association is told in stained glass, with memorials to Booth, Jefferson, John Drew, Richard Mansfield and Harry Montague, all communicants during the golden era of the theatre. From Lester Wallack's pew the nave stretches in intimate beauty to the chancel rail, under a low and fretted ceiling of polished wood. The Florentine red of the St. Faith window, dating back to the Napoleonic Wars, casts vermilion shadows on the gleaming brass of the pulpit. The altar, white in a sombre setting, tells the story of the Trans-figuration in Caen stone, and the windows at either side flood the chancel with their soft, antique green light.

Many who steal into the church for a quiet hour believe that there is something ageless and eloquent about the Oberammergau crucifix, the St. Faith window, the mediæval carving from a Scottish monastery now in the brides' altar, the Venetian mosaics, and the laces and opal-studded vestments used for ceremonial occasions. All of the gifts in the church, from the engagement rings set in the tabernacle door to the tall, silver candlesticks in the mortuary chapel, have had emotional significance for the donors. The Lady Chapel, the second Dr. Houghton's memorial to his wife, is a small treasure house of exquisite workmanship on which he lavished years of care, and the brides who drop in to kneel at the *prie-dieu* before its altar find a rare devotion expressed in marble and mosaic.

While the city has grown up to The Little Church Around the Corner and miles beyond it, wedging it in on all sides, the *close* has remained inviolate, a grassy plot where shrubs, vines and spring flowers have continued to grow in the shadow of a fourteen-storey office building. All day long the strains of the Wedding March drift through the open doors, and the birds that nest in the tower toss bright cascades of melody on heedless ears as they splash in the tinkling fountain. Many noted brides have looked into the kind brown eyes of Michael Bellizzi, the verger whose long attendance on the church of romance ended with his death in the winter of 1930. Coming to the parish in 1907, Michael had established a record for the amount of rice and confetti he had swept up. He had seen fashions in weddings change, carriages giving way to motor cars, bustles to boyish forms, gold wedding rings to platinum, and long locks to bobbed hair, but the brides had remained the same in their determination to get married under the shady eaves of the Church of the Transfiguration.

Michael, hosing the lawn and working with his flower pots, was as much a part of the church as one of its stained glass windows. He lighted the candles on the brides' altar and attended to the ceremonial of the services. He knew the feel of every pew without a glance at the brass plate, and his holidays were spent from choice in the seclusion of the churchyard, for his work was a labour of love. He mourned the fact in recent years that the brides no longer walked through rows of Canterbury bells, peonies, roses and the bright blooms of twenty years ago. The dust and gasolene of the city had robbed his garden of much of its life and colour. Tulips, azaleas and rhododendrons still line the path of the spring brides, but privet, ivy and shrubs are the sole survivors in June, when the weddings are at their height. The green of the lawn never languishes, however, and on the hottest summer day the garden lies with the freshness of an oasis under its ancient elm.

Once, the *close* was filled with the trees planted when the church was founded. The little magnolia near the tower was the first to die under the stifling growth of the city. Two of the three elm sisters went in turn, leaving a solitary survivor to spread a shady branch across the street. A snow storm in 1918 bowed the wandering limb so that it had to be cut down to let traffic pass. Tree surgeons doctored it and it now has a cemented side, like the ancient yew in Stoke Poges churchyard under which Gray composed the first draft of his elergy. But the brides rarely raise their eyes to the elm that still stands guard, thick with leaves in summer in spite of its wounded side, and frostily majestic under the icicles of winter.

Passersby are constantly drawn into the church by the charm of its *close* and the lich-gate, a wayside shrine on the pavements of a metropolis. Quiet figures linger in the pews, saying a prayer or lost in contemplation, and invariably there is someone back on a sentimental pilgrimage. More than two hundred visitors come and go in a day, and the book they sign in the vestibule is tinctured with the cinnamon and mimosa of distant places, for the tradition of the church has taken root in many countries. In addition to all the weddings there have been twenty thousand baptisms and twenty-five thousand funerals in eighty years. History has touched it in passing, and songs, poems, a play and several moving pictures have carried its tradition to remote and unlikely spots, so that to-day sight-seeing buses draw up at the gate to let visitors stroll through the twisting aisles of the church of brides and actors.

While it appears to doze most languorously in its quiet by-way, actually it is one of the busiest parishes in existence. Moss has not grown on its activity though an air of graceful age has settled on its gables. Life moves swiftly in the little office to the rhythm of Lohengrin, and weddings are still being solemnized when the vesper hour steals quietly over the church. Good Friday brings its solemn ritual and Christmas its snowy festivity. June ushers in a new assembly of brides, and the candles flicker softly in St. Joseph's for the passing of a soul. Sometimes as many as three weddings are in progress at one time, while the coved oak chapel under the tower harbours the dead. The sacraments of baptism and marriage are forever being administered, and its rectors have had the reputation of hearing more confessions than any clergymen in the city outside of the Roman Catholic Church.

Its activities have been strung together much like the church itself—a simple cluster of odd pieces growing without form or purpose, to assume at last a natural charm and to settle restfully into a shifting environment. Its cross is only forty feet from the ground and its towers are sunk in lowly silhouette against tall office buildings. Every seven years there has been restoration, but nothing has ever been torn down or destroyed. Each of its rectors in turn has felt that the character of the church must be kept intact. When Dr. Ray became rector he immediately made it clear that the old traditions would be preserved.

> It is our desire to continue The Little Church Around the Corner as the founder left it, a House of God where class distinctions are forgotten, the exemplar of everything that stands for love and charity among mankind.

Wealth and poverty, leisure and want have found a meeting place in its quiet interior. Twenty-cent tickets for beef stew have been handed out to the unemployed by a priest in biretta and cassock, dispensing twentieth-

THE LITTLE CHURCH

Imp R L B

R L Boyer

century charity under the lich-gate of the Middle Ages. The needy have fitted on new boots in the path of old parishioners, lavender and lace survivors of the Victorian tradition on their way through the churchyard to kneel in prayer before the altar. This is in keeping with the history of the church, a place of worship which has fostered liberality along with a strict adherence to form. Beyond the lich-gate lies a graceful unity of life, and although other churches, one by one, have moved uptown, Transfiguration elects to remain on its old site, an architectural anachronism in a green garden—just around the corner.

II

YOUNG FAITH IN OLD NEW YORK

THE peace and beauty that have dwelt with the Church of the Transfiguration for eighty years were the endowment of the founder, who came to New York from New England before the sleepy metropolis had caught the first faint signal of an imperious age of industry. Far below Twenty-ninth Street stretched the city, with tree-lined streets and friendly stoops. The turquoise arc of the noonday sky and the blue-black dome of night touched lightly on the consciousness of people who walked in open spaces and lived beneath lowly rooftops. Dewdrops fell like moonstones from the hollyhocks of Fifth Avenue at dawn, and the haunting perfumes of flowers drifted through side streets when twilight spread its soft maze of shadows over the city. Each man knew his neighbour and there was time for an exchange of courtesies. In its leisurely way New York still bore the fading imprint of Nieuw Amsterdam.

Fifth Avenue started out with swallow-tailed dignity at Washington Square but became a rustic path above Twenty-third Street. Broughams and victorias were jostled by straggling herds bound for the cattle-yards that stretched two blocks beyond Forty-fourth Street. A blacksmith shop stood across from the site of the Grand Central Terminal and there the horses were shod with the clank and shooting sparks of a village smithy. Over to the west were the rooftops of Chelsea and the rambling buildings of the General Theological Seminary. London Terrace was being built and close to the seminary was Chelsea House, where Clement C. Moore, sitting before a blazing fire of hickory logs in his library, wrote: " 'Twas the Night before Christmas."

South of the site where Dr. Houghton's church was to rise among shanty-strewn fields was Peter Cooper's house. On Sundays he could be seen walking to All Souls Church, a muffled figure distributing dimes in the manner of John D. Rockefeller. To the north lay the home of Robert Murray, the nucleus of the modern Murray Hill. The distant villages of Bloomingdale and Bulls Head could be faintly discerned on the horizon. A vista of trees and fields stretched for two miles to Yorkville, then a village with perhaps a hundred houses. The rest was mostly wilderness, except for a strip of cultivation where country residences were dotted in irregular sequence along the East River, their velvety lawns brushing the water's edge. Willows drooped on the river banks and tall elms waved their fronds, like green ostrich fans stirred by a passing breeze.

The stream of city life surged between Bowling Green and Union Square, and the tide of fashion reached its height at La Grange Terrace, Beekman Street, Lafayette Place, Bond Street and Washington Square. When the terrace was first built it seemed an extravagant gesture to conservative citizens, but by the late '40's some of the most distinguished New Yorkers of the day were hanging their toppers and mufflers in mansions on La Grange Terrace. John Jacob Astor and William B. Astor both had their homes on this short, select thoroughfare. Franklin Delano, an Astor son-in-law, and Mrs. Walter Langdon, an Astor daughter, lived in the vicinity, and Austin Ledyard Sands had added another to the array of homes typical of the social life of the period. Now and again, when the Terrace was deep in snow, Washington Irving might be seen ploughing his way through the drifts to visit a relative who lived in the neighbourhood. His own home was at Seventeenth Street and Irving Place.

Joe Jefferson, who was to give Dr. Houghton's church its popular name, was beginning to attract attention as a comedian. Longfellow, Hawthorne and Poe were being widely read, and James Fenimore Cooper was in his declining years. It was a church-going, and God-fearing era, with every pew packed on Sunday. There was no greater counter-diversion to church than a walk around the new reservoir at Forty-second Street, from which the Palisades, Long Island Sound and the distant hills of Westchester could be seen. The motor car and the bicycle had not yet disturbed the serenity of the Sabbath, although the streets were noisy with the roll of carriages. St. Bartholomew's, at the corner of Great Jones Street, and St. George's, on Beekman Street, rivalled Grace and Trinity with the brilliance of their weddings.

This was the New York to which a lad of fourteen, dreamy and romantic, found his way from a rigorous background of piety and hardship. George Houghton was a poet during those early days in the glamorous city, but as time went on this strain was directed to an idealism that expressed itself in practical deeds. In later years he was to stand distinguished among his colleagues for the charity, tolerance and simple godliness of his ministry. His early training had paved the way for his choice of a career. He was born in Deerfield, Mass., on the first of February, 1820, the son of Edward Clarke Houghton, who was descended from Willus de Hocton, an English manor lord of the twelfth century. Years later his nephew and successor revived the feudal coat-of-arms *Malgré le Tort* and used it symbolically in the church.

The elder Houghton died when George was a child, and his wife, Fanny, had a struggle bringing up her three sons and one daughter. She moved with them to Pittsfield, and there she sewed, taught and rented rooms to make a living. She was a pious woman with a touch of granite in her nature, a Congregationalist who made her children go to church with unfailing regularity and prayed that George would take up Holy Orders. Looking back over the years he saw a certain inevitability about his choice of a career:

> Early my tottering little feet were planted in the Puritan paths and sedulously was I taught to walk therein. With Saturday's sun the week was done. Up into the cupboard went the playthings, down came the Westminster Catechism.

When Frederick, an elder brother, came to New York, George soon followed, although young to leave the family roof-tree. The city was a place of brilliance and fascination for the unsophisticated boy. He frequently walked from the Battery to such suburban regions as the Thirties and the reservoir. Carriages rolled past him, bearing lovely ladies in sprigged muslins who held diminutive parasols high above their heads and refused to let their spines relax, in spite of the jolting of the carriages on the cobbles. Men about town paid formal calls at 11 o'clock in the morning, dignified burghers with curled moustaches, striped trousers and tight coats heavily padded at the shoulders. They favoured chrysanthemums for *boutonnières*. It seemed to George a dazzling whirl, but he soon found that the gleaming disc of smart city life had a dingy obverse. He took to wandering through the squalid parts of town and this gave him something else to ponder over, for city slums were an equally novel experience to the thoughtful youth from New England.

The Five Points was notorious, and vice and poverty went hand in hand in this part of town. The streets were overrun with gambling dens, saloons and houses of ill-repute. It was rough and tough, and the ward-heelers and gamblers were as assertive in their operations as the bandits and racketeers of to-day. Straight from his thin-drawn and colourless background, George found the pattern of city life an absorbing and oddly-woven embroidery that repaid close observation. The theatre was a synonym for hell to him and, although he was destined to link the stage and church in a lasting bond, his one visit to a playhouse was made at this period of his life. Wandering about on the lower East Side one night with his cousin James, he was lured into the pit of the Chatham Street Theatre on a dare. There is no record of what the boys saw by the light of the flaring gas jets, except that George, with a touch of sanctimony, described it later as a "miserable, low, wretched comedy." Half an hour sufficed to disgust him with the "Piece and the Place." He never entered a theatre again. The reaction to his playgoing was instantaneous in New England, however. The two mothers exchanged horrified letters and George was scolded for turning to the world for enjoyment. Mrs. Houghton feared that the gay city was having its effect on her son. The facts were that he was living a quiet and studious life. He passed his nights in study of the classics and mathematics. In the daytime he worked in George C. Sheppard's shop at 591 Broadway.

While preparing himself for the university, he taught at Tarrytown Academy. It was rare in those days for a youth to work his way through college, but young Houghton supported himself by teaching while he attended the University of the City of New York. He was graduated with honours on July 20, 1842. There is scant record of what he did and thought during those early years for, although his quill was always dipped in ink and romantic verse frequently flowed from its point, little of his composition has survived. He and a friend edited and published a small magazine *The Iris*, and George fluctuated for a time between his theological and literary interests. His imagination was captured by the verse and prose of contemporary writers. He was also finding mental stimulus in the classics, and his sermons in later years were liberally sprinkled with quotations from Homer, Virgil and Aristophanes.

On his arrival in New York he had not attempted to join a Congregational Church but had attended the West Presbyterian Church. In the year of his graduation, stirred by the Oxford movement which was sweeping England, he became a communicant at St. Luke's Episcopal Church. There were many distinguished figures in the pulpit at this time and he had been going the rounds, sampling the theological fare in different churches, but with mental reservations and a keen eye for humbug. At St. George's he found the first Dr. Stephen H. Tyng, a preacher so popular that, according to a commentator of that day, he could walk from the pulpit to the door on the heads of the people. His eloquence made even Henry Ward Beecher hesitate to precede or follow him at public meetings.

Dr. Houghton and he were to stand in friendly fashion for two distinctly different points of view in the Episcopal Diocese of New York. Dr. Tyng was an avowed opponent of High Church tendencies, whereas the youth from New England was already beginning to foster the Tractarian movement in his own small circle. By this time he had definitely decided to abandon a literary career in favour of the church. By autumn he was taking the stage coach to College Point to study theology under Dr. William A. Muhlenberg, a scholar and preacher who fostered æsthetic ritualism. His finances were still a matter of concern, so, to swell an empty pocketbook, he taught Greek at St. Paul's College, an advanced school for youths conducted by Dr. Muhlenberg at Flushing. While at the seminary he came under the influence of some of the notable theological scholars of the day, Cruse, Hawks, Wainwright, Seabury and Passmore.

His trips to town were infrequent but he kept in touch with his two closest college friends, George Henry Moore, who was studying law, and Marcus Lorenzo Taft, who had chosen medicine for his career. All three were in the same boat, ambitious youths straitened for funds. Moore worked in his spare time as a librarian and Taft did tutoring and copying. He was gifted as a copyist, and young Houghton would give him his illegible verses, translations of the Attic poets or Latin hymns of monastic origin, to be carefully printed into a notebook which he kept. At the same time the seminarian wrote for periodicals and sent his verse to the magazines of the day, but there is nothing to show that his poetry was as well received as his prose.

Ninety-year-old letters, yellow and crackling like the dried-up leaves of an autumn past and gone, give a glimpse of the friendship that existed between the three young men, and reveal something of the romantic side of Dr. Houghton's youth. At one stage he decided to become a celibate and take up missionary work. Moore advised him "to leave all these dreams of self-immolation, abjuring the world, or regenerating it by any Jesuitism," warning him that he was not strong enough to stand the rigours of missionary work. At the same time Moore prodded him gently for his interest in the High Church movement, writing: "Your furious assault on our Puritan ancestry, and your unqualified admiration of that canonization of Laud by Newman, quite alarmed me." But there was no stopping the youth in his flaming adherence to a cause that had made little headway on this side of the Atlantic. In the autumn of 1845 young Houghton was ordained in the Church of the

Holy Communion, where Dr. Muhlenberg had just become rector. A year later he was advanced to the priesthood, but he continued for another year as a curate with his old mentor, before casting out on the tide by himself in the winter of 1847, when he was twenty-seven years old.

His letters of this period contain a faint note of satire for the outward show that prevailed in some of the churches. On Easter Sunday he found a multitude of "Medes, Persians and dwellers in V Avenue" at Holy Communion for the "usual fancy service." He was having trouble finding himself. Alone and friendless, with an unimpressive pulpit delivery, he had little outlet for his gifts, and an experience he had had at Trinity had not been flattering. It is recorded in his diary that "inadequacy of voice, it seems, prevented my success with regard to Trinity." And then he added, in philosophic vein: "I have no friends. Why then not trust in the Lord? For it is better than to put any confidence in Princes."

But the young priest was already studying the aspects of life that were to dominate his ministry. He turned readily from the suave Christianity of the wealthy parishes to the needs of the poor, the sick and the sinful. In this era "sin" was a well-defined social condition that had its expression in dens of vice and the lurid poster effects of the '40's and '50's. He was now a regular visitor at Bellevue Hospital, whose sick in those days were nursed by prisoners from Blackwell's Island. There were no chaplains to minister to the dying, save an occasional volunteer. In the squalid tenements of the East Side and the tumble-down wards of Bellevue, young Houghton conceived an abiding pity for the misfortunes of his fellow men. He abandoned his dreams of literary distinction, of monastic seclusion, and set his heart on a parish among the poor. It was something that had to be founded, and he cast about for a way to combine his Anglo-Catholic leanings with an open-handed and informal charity. He had no clear view of the road on which he was setting out, and never dreamed that fame would settle on the church of his creation.

III

LOVE LANE LEADS TO THE LITTLE CHURCH

FEW churches have come into being as simply and with as little promise as the Church of the Transfiguration. A young curate without influence or money was invading a well-tilled field and the more experienced preachers felt that his enterprise would fail. His notion of a little parish that would minister to the poor and would avoid worldly display was novel to the church traditions of his day. He first broached the subject to Arent S. de Peyster at the tea table one afternoon and succeeded in interesting him in his ideas. Mr. de Peyster enlisted the support of Dr. Lawson Carter, an aged friend who lived at 48 East Twenty-fourth Street.

The plan went into operation in a thoroughly rustic setting. Love Lane was one of the few roads that crossed Manhattan Island at that time. It ran from the village of Chelsea to the Bloomingdale Road and on towards the East River. In 1848 it ran to the south of Dr. Carter's grounds and it was along Love Lane, appropriately enough, that the first parishioners of The Little Church Around the Corner walked to worship through a coppery drift of falling autumn leaves and the amethyst haze of a wet October day. There were only six persons who had definitely decided to become parishioners, the de Peysters and the Woodhams, but they brought some friends along with them. When the young priest walked quietly to the pine wood desk that served for a pulpit he found a gathering of more than twenty in Dr. Carter's back parlour. His benefactor had given two rooms rent free for three months in the hope that he would be persuasive enough to succeed in founding his own parish. The congregation filled the larger of the rooms; the smaller became the chancel. To enter from Love Lane it was necessary to pass through a hole in the fence surrounding the vacant lot that adjoined the house.

A few school benches, a Bible, a prayer book, a wheezy parlour organ and the pine desk which served as a lectern, were the only appendages available for the youth who had been steeped in the ornate ecclesiasticism of College Point and the Church of the Holy Communion. He preached from the text: "The Church is Thy House" and the little group that had trudged through wet and muddy lanes to hear him were impressed with his sincerity, if not with his eloquence. He spoke haltingly in a low voice, fumbling at times for words. He was pale, and desperately anxious to evoke for his audience the vision that floated before his own eyes. He told them that he had no money and no possessions, but there was convincing forethought in the outline he drew of his plans. He hoped in time to have a suitable building, simple but commodious, where there would be impartial ministration regardless of the social standing, wealth or moral status of the individual. He would found one or more eleemosynary societies and take personal care of the sick, the poor and the unfortunate. And whatever course his parish should take, he added, the fullest observance of the sacraments and church ritual would be its guiding principle.

Outside the rain pattered against the window panes and the vista of fields was blurred and vague. The small congregation watched him with kindly appraisal but without much faith in his visionary plan. The pews of the Episcopal churches all over town were packed and comfortable, and the poor were apt to go elsewhere for their gospel. Even the church so humbly launched on this occasion was to take a turn that its founder did not anticipate. Preaching an anniversary sermon in 1864, when his parish had already achieved fame, Dr. Houghton looked back to this October day and said:

> As there was no unusual degree of self-seeking involved in this plan, not much beside an humble and earnest desire to labour for Christ and His poor—the location of the church and its charity were not designed to have been where the lines have since so pleasantly fallen to us, but on one side of the town, where those to whom it was the purpose specially to minister were mostly to be found.

THE HIGH ALTAR

imp R&B

R L Boyer

On the second Sunday, most of those who had come out of curiosity with the de Peysters and the Woodhams returned to their own churches, and the youthful priest was faced with a diminished congregation of fifteen. This was discouraging, but for seventeen months services were held in the two back rooms, and a wooden sign at the corner of Fourth Avenue and Twenty-fourth Street was the only intimation of the house of worship beyond Love Lane. Meanwhile Dr. Houghton continued his hospital work until the wards of Bellevue and the dingy rooming houses through the East Twenties became as familiar to him as the two back rooms where he preached. The parish was formally incorporated on February 12, 1849, as "The Church of the Transfiguration in the City of New York." Much thought had been given to the choice of a name and Transfiguration had been selected for three reasons. It was a name not already appropriated in the city; it commemorated an important event in the life of Christ; and, in the modest words of the founder:

> It seemed a fit appellation for what was then the least of the parishes, so few having been present with Christ on Tabor; and for a parish in which it was hoped that there might ever be the endeavour, as well as the desire, for that whiteness which none but the Heavenly Father could give —a parish which, if undistinguished for reflecting much of the glory of Tabor, might not be altogether so for fulfilling in some measure to the afflicted its associated ministry of reliefs.

Dr. Houghton stubbornly resisted the plan to build on the present site. He considered it too near Fifth Avenue and too far from the quarter where his ministry was most needed. Although the corner of Twenty-ninth Street was still under grass and there were few houses above Union Square, it was becoming increasingly apparent that fashionable homes would be built eventually at this northerly point. However, he was overruled by his vestry, and in the spring of 1849, three lots, Nos. 5, 7, and 9 East Twenty-ninth Street, were bought for $2,800, ten per cent of the purchase price being met by money from friends and members of the congregation. In the following November the Building Committee arranged for the church to be built at a cost of $1,900, not including the pews. Later on, Dr. Edward Delafield bought the remainder of the present site and held the lots for five years. When the parish was in a flourishing condition he sold them back, having given the church the use of the land until it was sufficiently prosperous to buy it from him. The rectory became the personal property of Dr. Houghton. The entire parish plot was 100 feet deep by 175 feet wide.

It became apparent before long that the original plan for a free church would have to be modified if the work were to continue. The vestrymen and wardens were all practical business men of their day and they persuaded the young rector that there must be some rented pews, with as many as possible free for those who could not afford to pay for seats in church. The building which was put up during the ensuing months stands to-day as part of the nave. It formed the nucleus for the haphazard architecture that was to characterize the Church of the Transfiguration as time went on. It was actually about one-fifth the size of the present edifice, a slender, chapel-like structure running east and west, near the northern boundary of the grounds. No architect lent his skill to the plain one-storey building measuring seventy by thirty-five feet; no spire arose to mark it a House of God. It was a commonplace temple reared in green pastures without marble or stained glass. The side walls were only twelve feet high and the ceiling made no pretension to loftiness at thirty feet.

The interior was as plain as the outside. At the west end was a gallery, which was later removed, leaving room for a small parlour organ and the quartette that preceded the surpliced choir. Trees and shrubs were planted and the church was at last ready for its formal opening. There was not another building on the block. The view was unimpeded down to Potter's Field and Madison Square, where smoke curled lazily from a few chimney pots. A small blue notice was distributed among the worshippers in Mr. Carter's back parlour, informing them that their new quarters uptown were ready for occupation.

LOVE LANE LEADS TO THE LITTLE CHURCH

The congregation of this church will occupy their new edifice in Twenty-ninth Street between Madison and Fifth Avenues on Sunday next, March 10. Service to commence at half past 10 A.M. Afternoon service at half past 3 P.M. The pews will be let on Monday in Easter week.

March 5, 1850

ABEL T. ANDERSON

ARENT DE PEYSTER

J. W. EDMONDS

ALONZO A. ALVORD

March 10 was a different day from the dismal autumn morning of drifting leaves on which the little band of worshippers had first met. There were now forty parishioners in all, and they walked, prayer books in hand, into the new church on a sunny morning with the early promise of spring in the air. Miss Sarah M. de Peyster, daughter of the vestryman who had helped the young curate to found his parish, was the first communicant. The poet from New England had found his moorings. Life flowed in on him in a rich tide as he preached his first sermon in the Church of the Transfiguration.

But the opening of the church caused scarcely a ripple in the Sunday calm of the city. Most of the parishes were clustered to the south of this daring experiment on the outskirts of town. The bells of Brick Presbyterian Church summoned the devout Calvinists to prayer and the chimes of Trinity flooded Wall Street with rippling melody. The church parade flowed in a dozen different directions on Sunday morning. St. Marks-in-the-Bouwerie was already rich with tradition. Grace Church was attracting a fashionable throng and Dr. Henry W. Bellows was at the height of his ministry at the Unitarian Church of All Souls. There were 290 clergymen and 19,000 communicants in the Episcopal Diocese of New York.

Sunday was a day of rest and profound quiet. Once the church parade was over, the blinds were drawn for the afternoon. But going to church was a ceremony in itself. Chains were stretched across the streets when the crinolined beauties and their top-hatted escorts had filed into church. This was to prevent the roll of carriages and the clopping of horses' hooves from disturbing devotions. The barriers were drawn back as the doors were flung open and the worshippers paraded out, chatting in friendly fashion. Evensong was as well attended as matins. Gaslight was still a novelty and the lamp-lighter was an object of interest as he made his rounds, touching to life the jets that turned window panes to squares of gold before curtains were drawn and the rippling reflection was blotted out.

The other side of the picture was different and Dr. Houghton knew it well. For many months he had been moving freely at all hours of the night and day through the Five Points, where squalor, vice and ill-health flourished with a Dickensian flavour. The decayed tenements of the lower East Side and their accompanying evils gave preachers a constant theme for their sermons. The houses and alleys were as sinister as their names and the misshapen figures that slouched through them. The rector of the Church of the Transfiguration moved fearlessly through the crooked lanes—Little Water and the leering alley known as Cow Bay. Before the Rev. Lewis Morris Pease and his wife opened their Methodist Mission on Cross Street, he had heard the dying confessions of men who had been stabbed and shot, had given consolation to weeping prostitutes breathing their last, and had brought food and clothing to starving children. There were nightly brawls close to his own front door between the residents of two rows of tenements on Twenty-second Street. The Episcopal Church had little contact with this phase of life but Dr. Houghton had announced at the start that his ministry would concern itself with the darker side of city life. Surrounded by various social eddies and a thin strata of snobbery, he quietly reiterated from the pulpit that his credo would be: "Fides opera."

> Faith and works is the motto of our parish: they laid
> the foundation of our commencement, they will rear and
> cement the coping stone of our completion.

The path was uphill. The pews did not fill at once and financial difficulties hampered the work. But tolerance and charity already abode in the humble interior of the little church. Twenty communicants were added to the congregation in the first year, so that by March, 1851, seventy persons were worshipping at Transfiguration. In the following May the use of the daily service was introduced. By this time Dr. Delafield, one of the earliest benefactors of the church, had bought the adjoining lots to the west. A school house had been built and a parish school opened with twenty-four boys already in attendance. By June, 1852, the congregation had outgrown the church and more pews were needed. It was decided to furnish the school-room with pews and make it part of the main edifice. A low, dormer-shaped storey was built above the former school-room and classes were transferred there. This was the beginning of the form of enlargement that has been characteristic of the Church of the Transfiguration and has given it a picturesque quality. Every few years there has been an adjustment to meet some immediate need. In this way it has acquired the intimacy of well-loved and well-worn possessions. The ground plan lies much like a carpenter's square, the long arm skirting the northern boundary of the grounds. As the building rambled in different directions it came to be known as the Church of the Holy Cucumber Vine. Its whole history has been one of spreading homeliness, odd gables and nooks that have been necessary and therefore in perfect harmony. The transept was built in 1854 and in the autumn of that year the church in its enlarged form was re-opened and the founder was formally inducted rector. Two years later the congregation gave the iron fence which encloses the property to this day and is as characteristic of the church as its fountain and lich-gate.

The interior was now beginning to acquire warmth and grace from the gifts of its parishioners. Stained glass windows of the simplest kind cast opaline tints on the congregation at matins, and flooded the pews with violet and old gold at the vesper hour. Dr. Houghton preached from a carved black walnut pulpit given by C. V. A. Schuyler, a vestryman, in memory of his son. F. E. Siffken matched this with a lectern of carved wood. In due time the pulpit was replaced by one of Carrara marble and wrought brass. The old font bearing the inscription: "One Lord, One Faith, One Baptism," was given to the church about this time. It now has a wealth of association about it from the number of noted babies christened at its bubbling stream.

At the close of the decade there was a further addition to the building and two years later the transept was extended and the library, now the sacristy, was built. Then the organ chamber was installed and the old bellows organ gave way to a pipe organ. In 1862 the first of the many memorial windows which adorn Transfiguration was installed by Mrs. William Cairns in memory of her daughter, Mrs. Richard S. Willis. Two years later the building was again enlarged and new pews were added. In 1863 the Transfiguration window, a copy of the Raphael in the Vatican, which now sheds its lustrous colouring on St. Joseph's Chapel, was placed above the high altar. By this time the church had assumed the general outlines of to-day, with seats for more than a thousand worshippers.

During this period of early growth 438 persons had been baptized, including many whose names were to be well known in the life of the city later on, 356 had been confirmed, 100 buried and 200 married. The charitable societies, on which the young rector had set his heart, were well established and the parish was synonymous with kindly deeds. In his anniversary sermon, fourteen years from the day on which the church doors were opened, he reviewed the period with less regret over the site that had been chosen, for he had found that his charity had not suffered by proximity to Fifth Avenue.

But to what, humanly speaking, for all we know is of God, are we to attribute this growth out of nothingness and namelessness, this improbable prosperity, this contrast of to-day with the day of our beginning? Doubtless the fair place and goodly heritage wherein our lines have so pleasantly fallen, were not without their influence.

For the early '60's had brought wealth and fashion to the doors of the church and the pews were filled to overflowing at every service.

IV

TRANSITION DAYS

THE rector of the Church of the Transfiguration had definitely established himself during the '50's as a personality in the church life of New York, chiefly for his charity and his personal ministration. He was by no means a smooth-tongued orator who could match words with some of his brilliant contemporaries. Everything he had to say was written out in advance and he rarely alluded to current problems. He confined himself to the scriptures and emphasized the sacraments. His voice was low-pitched and his bearing gentle. He was a man of medium height who moved with dignity in heavy vestments. His hair grew back from a high, thoughtful forehead and fell in thick locks around his neck in the fashion of his time. His crisp, brown beard was trimmed close to his chin, unlike some of his fellow divines, who had patriarchal beards or straggling whiskers.

In the first year of his ministry he made his home and study in a room in the church, and there he lived with such simplicity and abnegation that he spoke of himself as the *Hermite* in letters to his old college friends. When the General Theological Seminary decided to add the study of Hebrew to its curriculum Dr. Houghton, who was one of the best Hebrew scholars of his day, accepted the post at a salary of $500 a year. A little later he was able to leave his monastic cell for more comfortable quarters, but he continued to teach Hebrew until the summer of 1863, when his church was flourishing. And so, to quote his own words, he "did not eat the seed corn needed for planting, did not take as salary for maintenance the money required for foundation laying."

It took the young rector several years to emerge from the financial difficulties that beset him in the early days of the church, but up to the time of his death he contributed constantly to the endowment fund, which was launched at his own suggestion. For twenty years he was the third largest contributor at Christmas and Easter to the general charities and funds of the parish. The amount usually exceeded one-half of his income, and in one year at least it exceeded the whole of it by several thousands of dollars. His salary was always more or less problematical, depending on the budget of the church. The first record of any remuneration is a vestry note dated February 1, 1855: "Resolved that the salary of our rector be fixed at $2,500 per annum, to commence the first day of Feb. instant."

At that time he was living with his young niece, Anna Houghton, in a little wooden cottage on the south side of Twenty-ninth Street, just across from the church. She was a mere child and not yet old enough to assume any of the parish duties, but after the death of his wife she returned to keep house for him. For many years the small and vivacious Miss Anna presided at the rectory and helped her uncle with his charitable work. When her brother, the second Dr. Houghton, was installed in the church, she went abroad to live. She kept in touch with the parish and returned for his funeral. In the summer of 1930 she died in Nice, well on in her nineties, the last Houghton link with the church.

Shortly after he founded Transfiguration the rector met Miss Caroline Graves Anthon, a relative of Charles Anthon, professor of Greek and Latin at Columbia College and a well-known scholar of his day. The Anthons were all Low Church and did not altogether approve of the ritual at Dr. Houghton's church. Miss Anthon, who was in her early forties, taught drawing at Miss Callender's school for girls and devoted much of her time to art. She and Dr. Houghton were married on October 9, 1855, by the Rt. Rev. Horatio Potter, who had become Bishop of the Diocese of New York the year before. During the days when the church was attaining its early fame Mrs. Houghton presided at the rectory, two of her unmarried sisters living with her for several years. Her husband paid her a unique tribute by having the illustrated

Imp RLB   R L Boyer

THE REVEREND DOCTOR GEORGE HENDRIC HOUGHTON
    FOUNDER AND FIRST RECTOR

Compline Psalms, which she had done on parchment, reproduced in stained glass and installed in the church as a memorial when she died in 1871. Her handiwork may still be seen in the Elizabethan window overlooking the nave.

Among Mrs. Houghton's closest friends was Miss Ann Aurora Ballow, who conducted a smart school for girls which Miss Keeler, the first bride of the church, attended. Another of her intimates was Mrs. Gerardus B. Docherty, wife of a genial professor of the New York Free Academy. They were all interested in the church societies, and meetings were frequently held at the Docherty home on Thirty-first Street, east of Madison Avenue. Dr. Docherty was junior warden of the church and he would drop in on the rector during the afternoon to discuss parish affairs, a call or a formal note being the favourite means of communication during this era. The good professor was one of the picturesque figures of the church in its early days. He was much beloved and a scholar of parts. It was his custom to sit at the end of his pew resting his bearded chin on a hand adorned with a large diamond ring. Its glitter was of so much interest to the members of the boys' choir, who used to sit on a long bench at the north side of the chancel, that they could not take their eyes off it. Joseph Osborn Curtis was one of the boys hypnotized by Professor Docherty's magnificent diamond. He attended church with his father and his grandfather, and the altar flowers on Easter Sunday—the first to be put to this use in New York—came from the Curtis country place at Hell Gate. Their family pew was on the main aisle and well towards the front.

Joseph was also a pupil during the late '50's at the day school connected with the church and there, learning Latin roots with him, were John Alvord, Edward Bissell, William and Glover Arnold, Sperry and Vanie Kane, Henry Gillespie, the Zabriskie and Milliken boys, and Edward C. Houghton, a nephew of the rector. Edmund Burke was principal of the school, an excellent teacher in his day and one who was long remembered by his pupils. The confirmation classes were constantly growing larger, and a notation by Dr. Houghton in an old register gives an interesting side-light on the infant days of the church. In the middle of the confirmation service one Easter eve "the gas failed and we were obliged to go out for a supply of candles."

The church lost two of its best friends in the early '60's. Abel T. Anderson, the first senior warden and one of the earliest benefactors, died in 1862. It was he who had suggested building the church in such a manner as to leave open and unoccupied a large portion of the grounds. In the following May Mr. de Peyster, a founder and incorporator of the parish, was buried from the church he had helped to create. Many of the plans for its welfare were devised in his house and Dr. Houghton received his first encouragement over the tea cups in the de Peyster drawing room. It was under his direction that the church grounds were originally laid out, and the trees and shrubs were planted to suit his taste.

By this time they had grown to a goodly size. On sunny mornings the congregation worshipped with open windows and the fountain scattered rainbows on masses of sweet-smelling blooms. Hospitable to all comers, Dr. Houghton had installed bird houses in the trees which, while scarcely a match for old Bond Street's stately branches, were already throwing restful shadows on the church. The Bond Street trees had long been the pride and boast of those who felt that New York was losing its charm as it went racing northward like a hoodlum boy tired of a dignified home. There were two in front of each house, well-dressed sentinels, so tall and dense at the close of the '50's that from the street only the stoops of the houses could be seen. The lamps twinkled through the branches at night like the fairy lights of Vauxhall Gardens, which were even then being smothered by the onward march of the city.

The Church of the Transfiguration no longer stood in isolation. The congregation of Brick Presbyterian Church had moved north from Beekman Street to Fifth Avenue and Thirty-seventh Street. The new church was plainly visible to worshippers through the windows of Transfiguration, with only a house intervening here and there. The city was moving northward at an irresistible pace and mansions were beginning to line Fifth Avenue as far up as the Thirties. The elder John Jacob Astor had died two years before Dr. Houghton founded his parish, but several of the Astors had moved to the Thirties from La Grange Terrace in the meantime. Mrs. William Astor, the former Miss Caroline Webster Schermerhorn, had been married in Grace Church in 1853. When the two Astor houses were built at Thirty-fourth Street she and Mrs. John Jacob Astor became communicants at the Church of the Transfiguration. As *the* Mrs. Astor she was just beginning to assume her sway as social leader, and where she went others followed. After observing Dr. Houghton's work among the poor, and in the red light district, she gave him *carte blanche* with funds and became a generous benefactor of the church. While the fashionables of the day were pouring in through the *close*, the rector's charity was extending to the poorest and the most depraved. His night bell and speaking tube were responsive to every summons from hospital, prison, house of ill-repute or any place where the services of a priest were needed. He heard the confessions of the dying of all denominations and never stopped to ask what a man's creed was.

The '60's found the pews of the Church of the Transfiguration packed. In the records of births, baptisms, confirmations and weddings began to appear such names as Rhinelander, Gould, Pell, Draper, Arnold, Hurry, Guion, de Rham, Delafield, Biddle, Suydam, Betts, Sands, Kent, Vanderbilt, McVickar, Dana, Zabriskie, Milliken, de Peyster, Schuyler, Drexel, Alvord, Ballow, Sutton, Townsend, Embury, Quintard, Livingston, Peck, Roosevelt, Howland and Gerry. Emily and Helen Astor were in the confirmation class of 1869.

Fifth Avenue still maintained a decorous front behind its high stoops and railings, and the Easter parade toward the close of the decade was the spectacle of the year. The traffic jam was one of crinolines rather than motor cars, although the fashionable hoop was soon to surrender to the bustle. Small hats were tilted high on elaborate chignons, and fans and prayer books were carried with the smelling salts of a swooning generation. Whiskered gentlemen with Prince Alberts, choker-collars, stiff-bosomed shirts and top hats with curling brims, walked around the corner from their Fifth Avenue homes or drove to church in phaetons and broughams. Mrs. Astor did not use her famous horses for church-going but walked the five blocks to Transfiguration, and there were few who passed her by without knowing her identity.

The rapidly growing fortunes of old New Yorkers were paving the way for the social elegance of the '80's. There were profiteers and many purse-proud men of affairs. Brownstone fronts were steadily encroaching on the meadows and lanes that wandered up to Yorkville. Harper's was running Dickens, Thackeray and George Eliot. The velocipede was coming into fashion, and there was apprehension lest it should weaken church-going habits. All over town people were spending their time in a dizzy bicycle whirl at academies and rinks. Grace Church could hear the whizzing velocipedes in a building next door to its dignified spire. The Botanical Gardens, extending from Forty-seventh Street to Fifty-first Street, made a pleasant afternoon drive, cards being dropped for formal calls, while fringed parasols were daintily tilted against the sun. The Fifth Avenue Hotel had been opened under the management of Paran Stevens. P. T. Barnum, having launched Jenny Lind at Castle Garden at about the time Transfiguration was founded, now lived in an elaborate home at Fifth Avenue and Thirty-ninth Street. City Hall Park, like Vauxhall Gardens, was no longer the gay, glittering place with coloured lamps that it had once been, for it was now "down town." Battery Park was still a smart promenade.

During this period Dr. Houghton was quietly promoting the Anglo-Catholic revival in this country. Allied with his strong evangelical strain was a metaphysical interest in the Oxford movement, which was leaving an uncomfortable backwash in this country. It had had a profound effect on him in his student days and had moulded him to a point of view which eventually was to make his parish unique in New York for its combination of informality and punctilious ceremonial. Years earlier, John Keble had launched the Oxford movement with his sermon on National Apostasy. While Dr. Houghton was still in the Seminary, Cardinal Newman had joined the Roman Catholic Church and tracts were now reaching the rectory from England, setting forth the authority of the Anglican Church, claiming apostolic descent for the Episcopate and advocating the restoration of discipline and the maintenance of a stricter orthodoxy.

Every move made by Newman, Pusey, Keble and Froude was followed by Dr. Houghton and his imagination was stirred by the dramatic tideburst that was rocking the church. He was the first priest on this side of the Atlantic to stand emphatically for the Oxford movement and he succeeded in imposing the new order without embarrassing his congregation. Several of his contemporaries were condemned or ostracized for following the Catholic trend, and the Anglican Communion in England was being rent asunder for the time being, but he moved calmly on his way, elevating the ritual while he dispensed an all-inclusive charity. He was so much beloved that there were no serious consequences, although an occasional communicant frowned on the emphasis placed on ceremonial. One of the vestrymen thought he must leave the church if the use of the Processional Cross were introduced, but in the end he became a confirmed High Churchman.

Some of Dr. Houghton's pulpit colleagues deplored the ritualistic trend of the Church of the Transfiguration, while admiring the gentle charity of its rector. The Eucharistic Lights and the Altar Cross were the subject of controversy at a General Convention for which he had hospitably opened the doors of his church. One of the speakers grew excited as he observed the course of the service. "That Cross is leading the way, and those candles are lighting the way to Rome, sir!" he exclaimed. But Bishop Potter, a tolerant cleric who knew how to reconcile the different elements in his diocese, could see nothing inappropriate in the introduction of the two Eucharistic Lights in Dr. Houghton's church. When asked if he would not refuse his sanction, he observed: "On the contrary, I think that we make altogether too little of the things which teach through the eye." He warned Dr. Houghton, however, to consider whether he should run the risk of breaking his neck for a straw. The Bishop knew the temper of the diocese on this subject. There was another mild flurry in the church when Dr. Houghton asked his congregation one Christmas to kneel for the Incarnatus in reciting the Creed. Some did and others did not. Many years later, reviewing this period in an anniversary sermon, Dr. Houghton said:

> Forty-five years ago the sign of the Cross, the surpliced choir, candles, an Altar Cross, Eucharistic vestments, the Crucifix, the eastward position, kneeling at the Incarnatus, the reverent inclination to the altar, flowers, the preaching in surplice, the Invocation of the Blessed Trinity before the sermon, the saying of the Litany at a Fald stool and asking the congregation to rise at the presentation of the alms upon the altar—subjected one to more than remark. Now this is no longer so. What has been done and taught at Transfiguration and the manner of the doing and the teaching, have accomplished not a little in effecting this change.

The simplicity of Dr. Houghton's spirit saved him from the drift of criticism and went far to promote the Anglo-Catholic movement in this country. His church was packed to the doors with the socially elect of the day. Without raising a finger to bring them, preferring to spend his time among the unfortunates, there was something about his parish that had attracted all classes from the start. Even before it became The Little Church Around the Corner, it was a common meeting ground for persons of assorted interests and tastes.

V

THE NEGRO FINDS A HAVEN

Dr. Houghton was a champion of the Negro during the Civil War. While the draft riots raged in New York in the summer of 1863, he gave his protection to scores of refugees and put his life and his church in danger to aid the hunted Negro. When the rioting was at its height and the mob was stampeding through the streets, sacking, burning and beating people to death, he stood calmly at his iron fence, arm upraised, and dared the rioters to take one step within the glebe land where he chose to protect the black man. To this day a quaint memorial, the only one of its kind in a white man's church, may be seen near the transept door of The Little Church Around the Corner. It represents the baptism of the Ethiopian by St. Philip and is in memory of George and Elizabeth Wilson, "some time doorkeepers in the House of the Lord."

The Church of the Transfiguration was believed to be one of the underground stations for Negroes making their way from the south to Canada. At least it was known that Dr. Houghton was a sympathetic friend and abolitionist. Wilson, who had been a slave himself, acted as courier and go-between in leading the runaway slaves to safety on East Twenty-ninth Street. During the three days of terror when an insensate mob of thugs, gangsters and ignoramuses virtually took possession of the city, scores of Negroes gathered at the church and were given quarters in the parish library, the choristers' robing room and the school room above the chantry. The overflow slept in the nave.

All around the church the rioters swung their clubs, pitchforks, pokers and knives, a motley army with clumsy weapons thirsting for blood. Flames licked the skyline at a hundred different points. Ten houses were burned on Thirty-fourth Street and the battle raged all through the Twenties and Thirties. Negroes were dragged from their beds and hung from trees and lamp-posts. A Negro church in Thirtieth Street, close to Transfiguration, was burned to the ground. Drunken gangsters from the Five Points, the Bowery and the waterfront, battered down the doors of the Coloured Orphan Asylum at Fifth Avenue and Forty-third Street. Two hundred Negro children under twelve were quartered in the pillared Colonial building, a peaceful-looking institution behind its screen of sumach trees. As the doors gave way and the rioters trooped through, the children were hurried out the back entrance and taken to a police station. From there they were sent to Blackwell's Island under military escort. Balked and furious, the mob looted the asylum and then set fire to the building. Firemen who made valiant attempts to set up their hose were thrown out into the street where they could watch the dancing flames that were breaking out in different directions. All over town columns of smoke and streamers of fire marked the plundering trail of the mob. Three times, scattered groups gathered at the Church of the Transfiguration, and their menacing roar brought the rector to the gate. They told him the church would be torn down about his ears if he did not oust the Negroes. Some of the darkeys had been seen out in the *close* getting a breath of air in the early morning. At first Dr. Houghton was persuasive; then, for once in his gentle life, he lost his temper. Shaking his fist at the brutish mob he cried: "You white devils, you! Do you know nothing of the spirit of Christ?"

There was something intimidating about a churchman who backed up his charity with such courage. That same day Colonel H. J. O'Brien, of the Eleventh New York Volunteers, had been clubbed, stoned, stabbed and dragged back and forth over the cobblestones to his death not many blocks from the church. Armouries, police stations, public buildings and private houses were being burned and plundered, and the presence of so many Negroes on the little strip of land that Dr. Houghton chose to call his glebe, made his situation doubly dangerous. On that hot Tuesday in July when the rioting reached its height, a sergeant in plainclothes called to say that the mob which had been turned away would undoubtedly return and the police could no longer guarantee protection. He urged the rector to let his unhappy refugees loose in the street and allow them to fend for themselves. Dr. Houghton indignantly resisted the suggestion.

"Well then, we can't help you," said the sergeant. "Things have got beyond our control. The mob will tear the church down about your head."

"No, they won't," said Dr. Houghton with calm assurance. "They will never enter here."

"What's to stop them?"

"I shall stand in the door of the church. I don't think they will pass me."

Dr. Houghton told the awed sergeant that the altar of God was an asylum for a wolf in the Middle Ages, and that it should be so for the black man in the nineteenth century. Thus one man, armed with spiritual weapons only, stood between the frightened Negroes and a savage mob. The refugees huddled together in the church, not daring to approach the windows lest the rioters should see their faces. Among them was the old coloured nurse of the Curtis family, who had been brought heavily veiled into the church during the night from their home on Thirty-fourth Street. Other family retainers, whose employers feared that they would be dragged from their quarters and killed, were secreted in Dr. Houghton's church during that period of terror. The Rt. Rev. George Seymour, Bishop of Springfield, arrived in the evening to pass the night at the rectory and lend moral support to his friend. Streets were now barricaded, smoke curled from scores of fires and the roar of the scattered mob swelled like pounding waves on a rocky coast. The gibbering, drunken riff-raff spread through the streets like a deadly undertow. The Bishop and Dr. Houghton kept calm vigil together, expecting an attack and possible death at any moment. Morning dawned on a demoralized city and still they were safe.

"Such an experience," the Bishop noted in his diary, "makes men love each other."

Theodore Roosevelt was then a small boy living at 28 East Twentieth Street. His mother, Mrs. Theodore Roosevelt, also gave refuge to the unhappy Negroes, hanging the American flag over the house for their protection. On the third day the militia was in control and the rioting was finally quelled. The refugees at the church breathed freely again and were able to appear in the air and sunshine of the little *close* that had stood between them and death. Edward A. Quintard, a vestryman of the church and one of the founders of the Union League Club, came in from his country home especially to offer Dr. Houghton funds to feed and care for his *protégés*. Just before the riots broke out, a lame and starving dog with a rope around its neck had crawled into the church through an air hole. Dr. Houghton took this as an omen for the period of succour that followed. He kept the mongrel at the church for nine years until such terrible dog fights shattered the peace of his cloister that he was forced to get rid of it.

From the beginning of the Civil War the rector had taken an active part in relieving distress. When the first war hospital was opened in the city he volunteered his services, just as he had done years before at Bellevue. For six months he ministered to the dying until a paid chaplain was appointed, frequently reading the burial office by the side of the hearse in the street in front of the hospital. The war, which produced its profiteers, also brought hardship and poverty to many, and in 1864 Dr. Houghton instituted the first of the three bread lines with which the Church of the Transfiguration has met emergencies. Each of its rectors has had occasion to take this measure. The second Dr. Houghton started a bread line in 1907 after the panic of that period, and Dr. Ray followed suit in the spring and winter of 1930 to alleviate the distress and unemployment that followed the financial crash of the previous autumn.

Dr. Houghton's championship of the Negro cause was to bring the coloured people flocking to his church. Their devotion to him was implicit.

imp RLB   R L Boyer

THE RECTORY

They would come to the services, sitting by themselves at the back of the church, while the old parishioners, militantly sympathetic to their cause during this period, occupied the rented pews. Dr. Houghton would often pause on his way down the aisle to give his Negro followers a whispered welcome or to inquire about their welfare. After the riots the two Wilsons became distinctive figures at the church, and remained with it for thirty years, until they both died within a few weeks of each other. Elizabeth dusted and tended the building as if she owned it. They were a handsome pair, who had earned the affection of the parishioners, and George bowed Mrs. Astor and her contemporaries into the church each Sunday with a courtly inclination of his head. He looked like a figure in moulded bronze as he stood through the services, doorkeeper for the rector who had given refuge to his people.

Elizabeth died first, Dr. Houghton and her husband kneeling by her bedside. She was buried from the church. George, who had loved her dearly, died a few weeks later. They were missed from their accustomed places and in due time the "Swing Low, Sweet Chariot" window was installed in their memory near the transept door. Oswald Grant, another coloured man, succeeded to some of George's duties. Then one day a deformed Negro boy knocked at the rectory door and dumbly waited for aid. He was one of seventeen children, a starved and abused imbecile. His father had made him earn coppers by dancing and clowning in saloons. Puzzled as to what to do with him, the rector, who was his godfather, finally decided to keep him as a handy boy, to answer the door bell. He bought him a navy blue uniform with brass buttons and canary stripes. George was the proudest boy in New York as he admitted a constant flow of visitors to the rectory. He did not mend his ways overnight, however, and there were times when he was a trial to his gentle benefactor. He died in a home for incurables and was buried from the church.

For a score of years Dr. Houghton's visits to old darkeys in Hell's Kitchen and in upper Manhattan were more frequent than his attendance at the social functions of his parishioners. His night bell summoned him to hovels where dying Negroes babbled of their days of slavery and their experiences during the Civil War. The baptism of young Negroes was generally held at vespers, and the register of those days gives an inkling of the high-sounding names that rolled through the baptistery—Napoleon Bonaparte, Ulysses Grant, Queen Victoria, George Washington and Abraham Lincoln. Dr. Houghton strengthened the link made during the Civil War riots by starting various activities in the church for the Negroes. He established separate sewing schools for white and coloured children. He founded a guild for Negro women named St. Monica's, after the mother of St. Augustine. It corresponded to St. Anna's Guild and was a charitable organization that dispensed necessities among the poor. St. Monica's met as a Bible class every Sunday afternoon in the chapel and later on in the parish house. A special Sunday School for Negroes was run, first by a coloured curate and, as the years went on, by a white seminarian who at times had his hands full and was obliged to exercise muscular Christianity. The Rev. James D. Stanley, chorister of the church for a few years, was forced to quell one obstreperous youth by dragging him off the premises along with the bench to which he had firmly attached himself. In the midst of a Christmas carol practice, the young heathen persisted in howling at the top of his voice on one discordant note. The more he was chastised the louder he howled. Mr. Stanley ordered him out of the room but this did not work. Seizing him by the collar he dragged him, still clinging to the bench, to the head of the stairs and helped him on his way downward. This was effective in establishing discipline in the Negro Sunday School.

Dr. Houghton's parish had already become well known for its open-handed charity. The Transfiguration Guild, one of the oldest charitable organizations in the city, was now in operation. The church was open at all hours, with a priest in attendance night and day. Until the Civil War the dance halls and houses of ill-repute had been confined mostly to the Five Points, the Bowery, Water Street, Cherry Street and the alleys along the waterfront. But after the war the vice centre shifted to the Twenties, particularly Twenty-eighth Street, in the vicinity of Seventh Avenue. The town was wide open and crime and vice were particularly flagrant. Gangs and criminals overran the region known as Satan's Circus. This was the notorious Tenderloin, and the Haymarket was in lurid operation a stone's throw from the Church of the Transfiguration.

Denunciation of sin had reached a stage that was not touched again until Dr. Charles H. Parkhurst began a fresh attack in the '90's. Henry Ward Beecher, that eloquent preacher who had recently returned from delivering his five orations in England during the Civil War, was drawing great crowds. From the pulpit of the Plymouth Church in Brooklyn he was declaiming on the social problems of the day. Both he and the Rev. Dr. T. De Witt Talmage, the ascetic pastor of Brooklyn Tabernacle, made personal pilgrimages to Manhattan under police escort and acquired material in Satan's Circus for their sermons. Both of these men were admirers of Dr. Houghton, who had little to say about vice in the pulpit but who was, in actual fact, the confessor of the magdalens in his neighbourhood and had more first-hand knowledge of existing conditions than all the other clergymen put together. On one occasion Dr. Beecher attended anniversary services in Transfiguration. Another time Dr. Talmage dropped into the church unannounced and took a seat near the lectern. When Dr. Houghton had finished his sermon Dr. Talmage rose and read the Coronation. The congregation sang the old hymn with evangelistic enthusiasm.

It was largely through Dr. Houghton's influence that the community of St. John the Baptist, a religious society of women in the Anglican Church, sent three sisters to this country to establish a branch order for the rescue of fallen women. A midnight mission was established, and strange were the confessions whispered in Dr. Houghton's ear as he knelt by death beds in frowzy surroundings and gave aid and comfort to frightened sojourners. There was one he never forgot. It was long past midnight when he was called to her bedside. He found her dying and in great mental distress. She had been brought up in the Episcopal Church and had been a choir singer as a girl. She was now the keeper of the house in which Dr. Houghton found her. All her concern was for her daughter, lest she should follow the same road. Her despairing cries haunted the rector all his life: "Oh, my Saviour, my Saviour, do not forget me now that I am dying, though I have forgotten Thee so many years." He promised that he would rescue her daughter. The woman was buried from Transfiguration, the inmates of the house weeping over her bier. The girl was sent to a convent by Dr. Houghton and was carefully educated. Years later, when St. Joseph's Chapel was being built, a large sum of money came from the magdalen's daughter, who was now happily married and well-off.

There was no such thing as a holiday in Dr. Houghton's calendar. Year after year he stayed at the church through summer and winter and, when urged to go to the seashore he always said that his fountain was his favourite ocean and his garden the joy of his life. The tablet on the church door read:

This is none other than the House of God and this is the gate to Heaven
Whosoever thou art that entereth this church, leave it not without one prayer for thyself, for those who minister and for those who worship here.

In the summer of 1865 he was finally persuaded to go abroad, but upon his return he said: "There is no recreation that can equal the daily ministering to you, flock of my heart. The end! May it come if it please Thee O God, while Thy servant can still minister at that altar and speak from this place." His hopes were fulfilled for, when he died, years later, he had worked up to the end, and as he was passing on, his lips could be seen moving in the familiar responses of the church.

VI

"AN IMPORTANT CHRISTENING"

THE dawn of the '70's brought widespread fame to the Church of the Transfiguration and entered it upon the calendar of time as The Little Church Around the Corner. The pattern of church life was changing throughout the city. Dr. Tyng was still preaching at St. George's, which had moved uptown from its old site on Beekman Street. His son, the second Dr. Stephen H. Tyng, had recently founded Holy Trinity and was the stormy petrel of the pulpit. Both of the Tyngs were extremely Low Church and in 1868 the son was tried for behaving in an "unbecoming manner" by preaching in a Methodist pulpit. Although convicted and publicly admonished, Dr. Tyng went cheerfully on with his work and became prominent in the Moody and Sankey revival of 1875. St. Bartholomew's was about to desert its old site on Lafayette Place and the Rev. Dr. Henry Codman Potter, later to become bishop, was preaching at Grace Church and was fast becoming as popular as his uncle, the head of the diocese.

New Yorkers were still gossiping over that daring innovation, the elevated railroad, and were much taken with the advantages of their water supply from the Catskills. The new gas brackets given by Mrs. Astor were hanging in the Church of the Transfiguration, and carriages were becoming more of a traffic problem every Sunday. The telegraph had become such a firmly established institution that there was a great falling-off in the delivery of perfumed notes. The beaux of the period had a taste for lacy valentines and lachrymose verse, but their lady loves were well entrenched in the primness of the mid-Victorian era. Their blushing cheeks and downcast eyes were matched by the sobriety of their costume, and they dared not be seen on the street in any attire less bountiful than a high-necked, long-sleeved dress of dark cloth or silk, with a bustle, yards of braid and a tassel or two.

The Church of the Transfiguration was in the very heart of the theatrical district by this time. New Yorkers who danced the cotillion in the ornate ballrooms of Fifth Avenue, and had Shakespeare for nightly fare before the footlights, drove in their carriages past the friendly gables of the church on their way to the theatre. Although the stage was in its golden era and New York had brilliant stock companies, actors were still without much social standing in the community. The breach between the church and the stage was wide and militant. The reforming preachers of the day had linked the theatre with all the sin and on-goings of such elements in the contemporary generation as were not wholly committed to puritanism. By a single act of charity Dr. Houghton gave ecclesiastical sanction to the play-actor, as he was known at that time, and quite unwittingly made his church famous around the world.

Joe Jefferson had given his first American presentation of Rip Van Winkle in 1866 and the part was now the current rage in the theatre. His bushy eyebrows, mobile features and large bow tie were known from end to end of the country, and wherever Jefferson appeared, the public flocked to see him. His stage career had started when he was only three years old. He had seen T. D. Rice play his blackface part *Jim Crow* in Washington and the fantastic figure had made such an impression on him that he "danced Jim Crow from the garret to the cellar." The comedian saw the shaver's imitation and was so taken with it that he blackened him in a miniature likeness of himself. He put little Joe in a bag and carried him out on the stage on his shoulders. After dancing and singing he launched his surprise with a couplet:

"O Ladies and Gentlemen, I'd have you for to know
That I've got a little darkey here that jumps Jim Crow."

The bag was turned upside down and out popped Joe Jefferson, making his début before his first audience. Twenty-four years later he was the leading comedian with Laura Keene's stock company and by 1866 he had attained a commanding place among the stars of the day. He was a friend of George Holland, an actor of excellent reputation but much less fame, who was now a feeble and aging player approaching his eightieth birthday. Jefferson considered Holland the merriest man he had ever known. His mere appearance on the stage before he opened his mouth sent audiences into fits of laughter. Of English birth, he had come to this country in 1827 and had made his début at the old Bowery Theatre. Jefferson got to know him in his declining years and in a fashion that made him apprehensive, for he had fallen heir to the rôle of the comedian in a play in which Holland was relegated to second place. It made no difference. The old man was generous to a fault and they became close friends. As prodigal as most members of his profession, he had fallen on hard times in his old age and during the season 1869–70, when the theatre was in a flourishing condition, he was penniless. Augustin Daly, who admired Holland, had just leased the Fifth Avenue Theatre and out of the kindness of his heart he gave the old man a succession of parts, including a rôle in *Surf*. He was so frail, however, that he crumpled visibly on the stage and Mr. Daly felt he must relieve him of his part and give him aid in some other way. He planned a benefit performance, which was held in the same theatre on May 15, 1870. The production was *Frou Frou*.

The aged comedian who, as Dogberry and Bottom, had brought laughter to three generations, moved his audience to tears that night as he stumbled out on Mr. Daly's arm between the first and second acts, unable to speak. He asked his friend to say for him: "I am, for the time being, no longer a low comedian, but a heavy blubbering father. Instead of quips and cranks, I feel myself better fitted for weeping." He took his curtain call with emotion and was unable to say more than "God bless you." Only a few months more were left him. He died in his sleep five days before Christmas. His home was at 509 Third Avenue, and Jefferson called to express his sympathy when he heard that the comedian was dead. Mrs. Holland and several members of her family went occasionally to the Church of the Atonement at Madison

Avenue and Twenty-eighth Street, and she decided that she would like the funeral to be held there. Jefferson and young Edward Holland, a son who was then playing at Wallack's, went to ask the Rev. William Tufnell Sabine, rector of the church, if he would officiate. The family links with the church were mentioned and it was pointed out that the dead man had been an Episcopalian. Mr. Sabine, obtusely enough, did not recognize Jefferson, although his face was as familiar to the public then as Charlie Chaplin's is to-day. In his autobiography, which ran serially in *The Century* in the year 1889–90, Jefferson recalled this scene as one of the memorable ones in his eventful life:

> On arriving at the house I explained to the reverend gentleman the nature of my visit, and the arrangements were made for the time and place at which the funeral was to be held. Something, I can scarcely say what, gave me the impression that I had best mention that Mr. Holland was an actor. I did so in a few words, and concluded by presuming that probably this fact would make no difference. I saw, however, by the restrained manner of the minister and an unmistakable change in the expression of his face that it would make, at least to him, a great deal of difference. After some hesitation he said that he would be compelled, if Mr. Holland had been an actor, to decline holding the service at the church.
>
> While his refusal to perform the funeral rites for my old friend would have shocked under ordinary circumstances, the fact that it was made in the presence of the dead man's son was more painful than I can describe. I turned to look at the youth, and saw that his eyes were filled with tears. He stood as one dazed with a blow just realized; as if he felt the terrible injustice of a reproach upon the kind and loving father who had often kissed him in his sleep, and had taken him on his knee when the boy was old enough to know the meaning of the words, and

told him to grow up to be an honest man. I was hurt for my young friend, and indignant with the man—too much so to reply; and I rose to leave the room with a mortification that I cannot remember to have felt before or since. I paused at the door and said:

"Well, sir, in this dilemma is there no other church to which you can direct me, from which my friend can be buried?"

He replied that "there was a little church around the corner" where I might get it done; to which I answered: "Then, if this be so, God bless 'the little church around the corner' and so I left the house. The minister had unwittingly performed an important christening, and his baptismal name of "The Little Church Around the Corner" clings to it to this day.

Although there are slight variations in the different versions of Mr. Sabine's refusal to conduct the funeral services of the aged actor, all the contemporary records agree on the essential points. Mr. Sabine gave a newspaper interview in which he said that he had a distaste for officiating at a theatrical funeral and "did not care to be mixed up in it." He admitted that there was nothing in the canons to preclude the burial of an actor from an Episcopal Church. He had always warned his communicants to keep away from theatres, however, as he did not think that they taught "moral lessons." When asked if he had recommended Mr. Jefferson to any other clergyman, Mr. Sabine said that he had told him he might go to the church around the corner for the funeral service. He had read in the newspapers that actors had been buried from Dr. Houghton's church. It was Mr. Sabine's recollection that Mr. Jefferson's observation was: "All credit to that little church."

In any event, without stopping to parley further, the two men walked hurriedly from Mr. Sabine's office to find the church around the corner where such things were done. Sitting behind a tall desk with many drawers was Dr. Houghton, kindly and ready for all emergencies. Forestalling a second episode like the first, Jefferson at once informed him that Mr. Holland had been an actor. The rector looked up at him with faint surprise and remarked: "I only know that your friend is dead and my services are asked. That is quite enough." He knew nothing then of what had happened around the corner. Nor did any inkling of the encounter with Mr. Sabine become public until after the funeral, which was held on December 22, 1870.

An hour before the services began, friends and admirers of Mr. Holland began to arrive in the dim hallway of his home on Third Avenue, among them Mr. Jefferson, Mr. Daly, Lester Wallack, Charles Kemble, Tom Barry, Lysander Thompson and Mason William Davidge. Mayor A. Oakey Hall was one of the pallbearers. The black walnut coffin was carried to the Church of the Transfiguration and was placed inside the main entrance. There was no mortuary chapel at that time, nor a lich-gate under which the cortège could pass. Old friends walked past the bier, illustrious actors of the day, and many of the lesser figures in the theatre, who had loved the benevolent comedian and had appeared with him in different productions. Dr. Houghton read the service and the actor was buried in Cypress Hills Cemetery in a lot belonging to the American Dramatic Fund, for he had little left when he died.

Next day, when the Church of the Transfiguration was wrapped in a sparkling mantle of snow and Christmas cheer abounded throughout the city, the newspapers carried the tale of Mr. Sabine's denial of burial rites to Mr. Holland. Indignation swept the country. The story travelled from coast to coast and was taken up in the leading pulpits. The opinions of clergymen were obtained pro and con, and even those most confirmed in their disapproval of the stage were inclined to think that Mr. Sabine had been uncharitable. A few rose to his defence on the score of inexperience but the prevailing note was one of sharp criticism and the effect was to give the maligned play-actor a recognition both social and spiritual that he had not had before. The newspapers, reflecting the public feeling, labelled Mr. Sabine a "canting Pharisee" and a current editorial gives an idea of the uncomfortable position in which the rector of the Church of the Atonement found himself:

> Mr. Sabine is an anachronism. He should have lived in the days when no harm was thought of using the rack and thumb-screws as a stimulant to a man's religious faith. If it is his lot to live in the nineteenth century he ought either to accommodate himself to its tone of thought or at least retire from a church upon which he brings discredit.

Dr. Houghton woke up to all this flurry and excitement with his usual air of quiet wonder that his parish should have been singled out for public attention. He had a recurrence of the indignation he had felt during the draft riots. Nothing was so foreign to his life and work as intolerance of any kind. He was amused by Mr. Sabine's patronizing allusion to his "little" church, since he had twice as many communicants as his neighbour on Madison Avenue. Both churches were filled to the doors on the following Sunday morning. People came from all over town to see the rector who had not hesitated to bury a stage favourite. But Dr. Houghton was not the man to rub in his charity and Mr. Sabine made no allusion to the episode. Transfiguration had now automatically become "The Little Church Around the Corner" in newspaper headlines. There was something about the name as well as the episode that caught the public fancy. In course of time the legend acquired such standing that it became necessary to use the secondary name on plaques at the church, in the telephone book, and in all notices affecting the parish.

Public approval of Dr. Houghton's act was expressed in a testimonial given on behalf of the dead actor's family. All of the scintillant stage figures of the era gave their services, including Booth, Lawrence Barrett, Jefferson, the Davenports and Clara Morris. The roster of the theatres that contributed to the testimonial is old New York's stage history—The Academy of Music, Niblo's, Booth's, the Fifth Avenue, Wallack's, the Olympic, Wood's Museum, the Bowery, the Fourteenth Street Theatre and the Grand Opera House. Holland's name became better known than it had been during his lifetime. A copy of the Bible illustrated by Doré was sent to Dr. Houghton from a Baltimore theatre. He discouraged various attempts to get up a testimonial on his own behalf, shrinking from personal notice. Chicago, however, insisted on holding one at Crosby's Opera House. At least 3,000 persons attended—"hundreds of ladies standing up and sitting upon the aisle floors"—no mean feat in the attire of the times. Men stood on the window sills, clung to stair railings and hung themselves up as wall ornaments, according to the records of the day. The proceeds were forwarded to Dr. Houghton with a note that they be used for the furtherance of that "exquisite commingling of Christianity and human kindness which our Divine Master taught, and of which we regard you as a noble exponent." He accepted the money in the spirit in which it was given and was soon in a position to return the courtesy. In the early autumn of the same year Chicago was swept by fire and on the following Sunday he asked his congregation to remember the "kindly folk" of that city. The gift was returned in full measure and was gratefully used for the alleviation of distress.

After the first stir had died down, little more was heard of Mr. Sabine. He was condemned by many of his own parishioners, who felt ashamed that such intolerance should have been displayed at their church. He did not retire, in spite of widespread denunciation, but joined the Reformed Episcopal Church and was a bishop at the time of his death. In due time his church was torn down to make way for a chemist's shop. It has long been forgotten except for its reflected fame from The Little Church Around the Corner, which grew stronger and more entrenched in its traditions with the passing of the years.

VII

IN SONG AND VERSE

THE Little Church Around the Corner had become the chosen sanctuary of the stage folk overnight. They paid Dr. Houghton the compliment of attending the services, and they elected to take their wedding vows at his altar. They brought their babies for baptism, and many burial services were read by Dr. Houghton for his friends, the play-actors. In four years' time the church was already referred to as one that had become noted in the history of theatrical funerals. The rector could look down from his pulpit and see the noble profile of Edwin Booth any Sunday morning. Joe Jefferson rarely missed a service when he was in town, and Lester Wallack, Harry Montague and Lawrence Barrett were all regular communicants. Mark Smith, who died abroad in 1874, was brought home and buried from the church and, four years later, it was Montague's turn. Hours before the services began the pews and the aisles were packed. Booth led the pallbearers, an impressive figure paying the last honours to a distinguished contemporary.

The church was chosen for Montague's memorial rather than the lobby of Wallack's Theatre, where it was first proposed that a bust should be placed in his memory. Wallack's passed on in time, but the memorial to Montague opposite the pew he used to occupy is one of the adornments of Transfiguration to-day. In warmly tinted cathedral glass he is pictured as a pilgrim with staff and scallop shell, and on a plate below is the inscription:

> If I ask Him to receive me will He say me nay?
> Not till Earth and not till Heaven pass away.

This was the first of the actors' memorials which now give the church a peculiar interest. The baptismal and wedding records of the period also testify to the theatrical following the church had acquired. Many of the names were glamorous in their day but are forgotten now. Others are familiar enough, even to ears attuned to sound pictures. A typical baptismal entry in 1873 shows E. H. Sothern, James W. Wallack and Kitty Chamberlain to have been the sponsors for Lester, son of Arthur Sewell. Rose Coghlan sponsored another baptism of the decade and Booth, Jefferson, Wallack and Barrett all appear repeatedly on the records as godfathers, or witnesses at weddings.

Although he remained the actors' friend for thirty years, Dr. Houghton never entered a theatre except for his one visit to the Chatham as a boy. Jefferson always hoped that he would go to see his Rip Van Winkle but the rector was consistent in his refusal to break his rule. Booth called on him one afternoon and asked him to accept a box to see him play Hamlet. His reply was characteristic:

> My dear Booth, I know that I would enjoy myself but while I am away from my little study here, some poor fellow may come in who wants a word of encouragement or a direction towards the light. I thank you, Mr. Booth, but my time is not my own. I have dedicated it to God and humanity.

Still living in great simplicity in his rectory and continuing his charitable work, Dr. Houghton watched the rapid accession of gifted parishioners during this period with faint surprise. His regular communicants, the old families that had settled in his neighbourhood, were proud that their rector should have done so simple and distinguished an act. Many of them were theatre-goers and great admirers of Booth and Jefferson. Taking a leaf from the rector's book, they began to invite the stars of the stage to their homes. A few, however, still regarded play-going as sinful and unchurchly. Although an ascetic himself, the rector of Transfiguration was no prig who believed good living to be a cardinal sin. His sermons would often contain quaint in-

꿈RLB   R L Boyer

THE ORGAN LOFT

junctions to his parishioners on the dividing line between worldliness and spirituality. His old manuscripts yield many of these excerpts indicative of his benevolent ministry.

> There is nothing amiss in having a coloured man behind the chair at dinner, and a dinner of terrapin and turkey, with something from God's vineyards to moisten them, and wearing gay clothing, and having a house on the Avenue, if God have given the means therefor, provided one proportion his alms—that which he gives to the poor —and his oblations—that which he offers to God for sacred purposes—to his estate.
>
> Many, many there are who need the Theatre, when that Place and its surroundings are what they might be, are what they should be, and what in many instances they are, and are more and more becoming. They need that Place for refreshment, for relief, for forgetfulness, for the brightening of a sometime dullness, for instruction, for the learning of many a good lesson, for the quickening sometimes to something better in the living.
>
> And so I say to those who count my counsel worth having: Yes, go to the Theatre, if the Place and surroundings be what they should be, if the play be proper, if the Actors be not men and women who are notorious for immorality, if the season be suitable and the evening be not that should be elsewhere and otherwise spent. Yes, go, if these things be so, but go with moderation.

In an era when the theatre was continually denounced from the pulpit, Dr. Houghton's kindly outlook brought him hosts of actor friends. Shortly after the Holland episode The Little Church Around the Corner began to be toasted in song and verse. The newspapers and magazines were swamped with poems. George Cooper, a popular song-writer of his day, composed the lyric which, set to music by D. S. Wambold, was sung in minstrel shows and did more to carry the tale of the Holland burial around the world than any other medium. Years later a play entitled *The Little Church Around the Corner* by Marion Russell, and a moving picture version, were to reach the Antipodes, but this was not until after the death of the first Dr. Houghton. For a generation the song was sung in variety. It was a slower business in those days for a song to achieve popularity, but the impression it made was lasting. Thus, people who never expected to see New York, sang the song dedicated to Dr. Houghton.

GOD BLESS THE LITTLE CHURCH AROUND THE CORNER

God bless the little church around the corner,
  The shrine of holy charity and love;
Its doors are ever open unto sorrow,
  A blessing fall upon it from above;
The rich and poor are equal 'neath its portals,
  And be our path in life whate'er it may,
No heart that needed comfort in affliction
  Was ever turned uncomforted away.

Chorus

God bless the little church around the corner,
  The shrine of holy charity and love;
Its doors are ever open unto sorrow,
  A blessing fall upon it from above.

God bless the little church around the corner,
  No matter what the Creed that it may bear!
However we may differ in opinion,
  The warmth of Christian sympathy is there!
A word of hope and kindliness awaits us,
  When clouds of sorrow hover overhead.
With needed words of pity for the living,
  And rev'rence for the cold and silent dead.

God bless the little church around the corner,
    And keep its hallow'd mem'ry ever green!
O, like a lily growing by the wayside
    It smiles upon life's ever busy scene!
It points the way to realms of joy unfading,
    And bears of love a never-ending store.
God bless the little church around the corner!
    God bless the little church forevermore.

Mr. Cooper composed a second song which he dedicated to Jefferson. It resembled his first one and became a parlour favourite, the chorus being arranged for soprano, alto, tenor and bass, in the fashion of the day:

GOD BLESS THE LITTLE CHURCH

God bless the Little Church! Where truth and love abound,
Where Charity and Peace and Christian Faith are found!
    The sorrowing and poor
    Have blest it day by day,
    And never from its doors
    The Dead are spurned away!

Chorus

    God bless the Little Church!
    God bless the little Church!
    Good angels fold their wings of gold
    Around the little Church!

These were the best known of the lyrics, but the Holland episode continued to be a favourite subject for contemporary poets, amateur and professional. George Vandenhoff was the author of a lengthy narrative poem which was read at Wallack's, the Fifth Avenue Theatre, the Academy of Music and Niblo's Theatre on the occasion of the Holland memorial.

THROUGH THE LICH-GATE

THE POOR PLAYER AT THE GATE

Wisely good Uncle Toby said,
   "If here, below, the right we do,
'Twill ne'er be ask'd of us above
   What coat we wore, red, black or blue."

At Heaven's high Chancery gracious deeds
   Shall count before professions,
And humble virtues, clad in weeds,
   Shall rank o'er rich possessions.

So the poor player's motley garb
   If truth and worth adorn it
May pass unchallenged through the gate,
   Tho' churls and bigots scorn it.

The Lord of Love, the world's great Light,
   Made Publicans his care,
And Pharisees alone demurred
   That such His gifts should share.

But still He held his gracious way
   Soothing the humblest mourner,
Nor ever bade one sinner seek
   For comfort "round the corner."

Some modern saints too dainty are
   To walk in paths like these;
They'd lock the gates of heaven on woe,
   If they but held the keys.

All honour to the little Church,
   And to its gracious Pastor,
Who in his heart the lessons kept
   Taught by his heav'nly Master!

And when this fleeting scene is past
   To sinner, saint, and scorner,
Let's hope we all may find, at last,
   A bright home round the corner!

IN SONG AND VERSE

As years went on, the verse written about the church changed in tone. Mr. Sabine was forgotten but the immediate beauty of the church, the flowers, the sanctus bell and the *close* inspired a fresh bouquet of verses.

THE SANCTUS BELL

By *Julia Pierson Mapes*

Above the din of toil, the City's voice
Of clangour harsh that grates upon the ear,
A silver bell resounds, distinct and clear,
Stilling men's turmoil, bidding them rejoice,
Goading their conscience, granting them no choice
Save that of turning to a belfry near,
The "Little Church" the world enshrines as dear;
It is her Sanctus bell, whose voice divine
Soaring upborne by angels from its tower
All fiery tongued with flame of heavenly power,
E'en mid earth's sin, still quickens heart of mine,
For our dear Lord bequeathed the Church's dower
That, pure in city mud, blooms music's flower.

THE LITTLE CHURCH AROUND THE CORNER

By *Florence Van Cleve*

O Little Church! I push aside the door
That keeps at bay the ravening city's roar,
And find here gentle peace and quietness,
Waiting to soothe the sorrowful, to bless
With silence the bewildered, storm-tossed soul.

The Happy Warriors who have reached their goal
Breathe benediction on me from the walls,
Where through the painted glass the sunlight falls—
"We fought the fight—we won the victor's crown;
Be not dismayed!" Like echoes floating down
From heaven, I hear the Happy Warriors cry.

THROUGH THE LICH-GATE

Still do they live, to succour such as I,
In these memorial windows; who can tell
How many led to heaven or saved from hell,
Were drawn here, Little Church, by your broad creed,
That knows no better law than human need?

I cannot come so near to God as now
Even on holy days, when many bow
Their heads in prayer; I crave this solitude,
Here for a moment's space my soul is free
And all the Happy Warriors pray for me.

My task is calling—calling; I must go;
With lifted heart, with reverent step and slow,
O Little Church! I push aside the door,
And with fresh courage face the city's roar.

THE LITTLE CHURCH AROUND THE CORNER

By Corie Davis Henton

Around the corner from the marts of greed,
  The money-changers' traffic and the rush
Of driving throngs, yet close to human need
  It stands, a shrine of peace and restful hush,
God's "Little Church" where Christ-like ministry
  That questioning not of race, or worth, or faith,
Sheltered black fugitives from slavery
  And freely sanctified an actor's death.

The day, subdued, through panes memorial steals,
  A Presence grave, serene, seems everywhere;
Stilled, comforted, the world-worn pilgrim kneels
  And thought becomes one deep unspoken prayer.

I think if Christ should come to earth today
Here best He'd love to go apart to pray.

{54}

IN SONG AND VERSE

GARDENS

By Stella Grenfell Florence

Here, in the garden of the Little Church,
Let us be still a moment—lose ourselves
In its delightful Old World charm, and dream
Of gardens shrined in History's yesterdays.

Man's destiny is interspaced with gardens . . .
The first man was a gardener. In a garden
(The fairest garden this world ever knew)
He walked a while—a little while—with God . . .
But, wearying of too much loveliness,
Aspired to heights beyond a mortal's ken,
And, so aspiring, infamously fell.

And in another garden Jesus trod
The winepress of God's wrath for all mankind;
Began His tragic journey to the Cross,
And sprinkled with His Blood the hallowed ground.

And in a garden He was laid to rest
After His Work was finished . . . There He slept
Until the dawn of that first Easter Day
Which witnessed His great triumph over Death,
And opened wide for us the Gates of Heaven.

And here, in the great city's restless heart,
Nestles this garden of the Little Church—
An oasis of beauty, love and peace;
A sacred shrine, commemorating all
The gardens that have helped to build our Faith.

Here that soft Voice that over Eden breathed
Its benison, may be heard; here, too, the prayer
That consecrated dark Gethsemane;

{55}

And here dwells that dear Presence that illumed
The garden tomb of Joseph . .   All are here!
And every leaf, and every blade of grass,
And every bird-note, thrills with loving praise
Of Him Who is the Planter and the Seed—
The Perfect Giver and the Perfect Gift.

Hundreds of other poems were written about Transfiguration as the years went on. Yet it neither sought its tasks nor worked for its fame. It was simply the little church of the open door where people walked in with their troubles and received practical and spiritual aid. Prejudice or sectarian feeling did not enter into its ministration and the prosperous members of the parish saw to it that there were funds for Dr. Houghton's charitable work. It was his boast that his church had a larger provision for free sittings than any other in the city and the pews were rented at a lower figure. There were a few critics in the diocese who reproached the rector for opening his doors so readily to the people of the stage, but his customary retort was that he would deny no living person entrance to the church, much less would he close the gates on the dead.

The Feast of the Transfiguration was first observed on August 6, 1873, and has since been regularly celebrated, with services adapted from the Sarum liturgies. This was the first observance of the Feast of the Transfiguration in the United States and eventually the date was entered in the Episcopal calendar as a result of Dr. Houghton's emphasis on the festival. He was among the first Episcopal clergymen in this country to advocate the recitation of prayers for the dead, and copies were placed at the church for general distribution, another Anglo-Catholic innovation that caused mild excitement in the parish.

VIII

A GOOD SAMARITAN

THE wedding tradition of The Little Church Around the Corner began in good earnest in the '70's. The brides of the day were extremely formal and an elopement was an event that shook society. Marriages were planned many months in advance, and fuss and feathers were indispensable to the ceremony. The spontaneous weddings of to-day had few counterparts in the rustling importance of the '70's, '80's and '90's. Many of the *point de Venise*, rosepoint and Brussels lace veils that still appear at the more conventional weddings are inherited from the grandmothers who belonged to this era. It was the custom to fasten the veil to the hair with a diamond star or butterfly, while cameos held the stiff satin folds of the bodice in place. Bustles, pointed basques and heavy jewellery were typical of the age. Bridesmaids wore frocks of forbidding lines with bonnets perched high on their coiffures in the Victorian manner, and tied under the chin.

One of the prominent brides of the decade was Miss Marion Graves Anthon, who was married to Stuyvesant Fish in The Little Church Around the Corner on a June day in 1876. She was a daughter of William Henry Anthon, the lawyer, and a relative of Mrs. Houghton. Most of fashionable New York trooped in through the sun-lit *close* to see Miss Anthon take her wedding vows. Later on she was destined to become a social leader who provided her generation with many sensations in the way of entertainment. She was one of the first to sponsor Mr. and Mrs. Vernon Castle, and they danced the maxixe and tango in her ballroom to the delight of her guests. Mrs. Fish gave her last dinner and dance in 1914, a year before her death, and on this occasion scores of canaries sang from wooden cages hidden in yellow groves of forsythia and jonquils. In the rush uptown she had moved from the old Fish residence on East Fifteenth Street, the scene of her most brilliant functions, to a modern home on East Seventy-eighth Street.

While she lived down town she attended The Church of the Transfiguration, and her children were baptized at the old font, as were many other babies whose family names are familiar to present-day New Yorkers. Mr. and Mrs. Elbridge T. Gerry were regular communicants and their daughter, Margaret, was baptized by Dr. Houghton. Another daughter, Mrs. F. E. Saxham Drury, continued to attend the church up to the time of her death in the autumn of 1930. Soon after the church acquired its stage following, the other arts began to view it with affection. Writers and artists were quick to appreciate its pictorial charm. Although it had no claim to architectural distinction, Stanford White used to drop in from time to time and his son, Richard, was baptized by Dr. Houghton.

While still maintaining its rural air behind the confines of its iron fence, The Little Church Around the Corner was now beginning to rub shoulders with a cosmopolitan world. The hotels, restaurants and theatres were all in the vicinity and the leading lights of the day, social and artistic, foregathered at Delmonico's, where Lorenzo and Charles catered knowingly to the town's *bon vivants*. Mrs. August Belmont lived four blocks farther north at Eighteenth Street on Fifth Avenue, and A. T. Stewart had recently built his marble house at Thirty-fourth Street. The first telephone book had been issued, a vest pocket affair containing only 252 names. Twenty-first Street was still one of the most fashionable side streets in town, while Thirty-second came next in popularity.

Toward the close of the decade, just as the city was about to twinkle forth in a jewelled network of electric lights, the heaviest shadow of its history fell on the peaceful parish of Transfiguration. It was a period of graft and financial scandals, and the newspapers were filled with the doings of the Tweed ring. Then one morning the parishioners of Dr. Houghton's church

Imp KLB   R L Boyer

IN THE CLOSE

were amazed to open their papers and read that one of the most prominent members of the congregation was being sought by the police for extensive forgeries of insurance scrip. He was a scholarly man, related closely to a leading preacher of his generation. After disappearing for a few days he gave himself up to the authorities and made a complete and amazing confession, explaining the mental processes that had led to his defections. Dr. Houghton, who was bowed down with grief over the episode, had urged him to make a clean breast of his guilt and had given him aid and consolation. He was sentenced to serve five years in Sing Sing. As the train pulled out of the station with the convicted man on board on his way to prison, he could still see the figure of Dr. Houghton standing on the platform watching him out of sight. That was in 1877. Attempts to have him paroled were unsuccessful and he served his full term.

The whole parish was in a state of turmoil, for no one in the church had had better standing in the community or had seemed more blameless in his habits. Dr. Houghton gave all the help he could to the man's wife and children. Preaching on the Sunday after his parishioner's conviction the rector, in a broken voice, alluded to the topic that was uppermost in everyone's mind. He made it clear that his friend had been living beyond his means in order to keep in the social swim, and he cautioned his congregation against extravagance:

> He was my best friend and trusted adviser. I have loved him and shall continue to love him in spite of all. Good people, if the means of any of you do not warrant a style of living consonant with the pace of the Avenue, I beseech you, seek less pretentious regions for your homes and pleasures.

Dr. Houghton had little taste for the social functions of his generation. His dearest friends were unable to lure him away from his study, but the poorest beggar on the Bowery could always command his attention. In one of his anniversary sermons he pointed out that the truth had never been withheld or modified at the Church of the Transfiguration lest any one of influence should take offence. All men were counted equal in his sight. His interest was rarely piqued by names. One day, when he was riding on an elevated train, the conductor came through and announced in great excitement: "General Grant is in the next car." Dr. Houghton looked up from the book he was reading. "I hope he is well," he said in a placid voice. This episode had its counterpart in his own church when the sexton walked down the aisle in the middle of a service and informed the rector in a whisper that Governor Hoffman was in the church. All those seated in the front pews heard Dr. Houghton's calm retort: "He couldn't be in a better place."

The church by this time had acquired a family of retainers and faithful adherents. Christine, a German girl who had recently arrived from Baden, was cook at the rectory, and a romance was blossoming between her and Ernest Diee, the French chef at the Calumet Club next door, a favourite haunt of the *gourmets* of the day. An exchange of clams for Dr. Houghton's supper had led to their meeting each other. Christine's assistants in the rectory kitchen sometimes received *billets doux* tied to lumps of sugar, which were dropped to them by waiters from the servants' quarters of the club. Christine was one of the busiest cooks in New York, thanks to her master's hospitality. The young people of the church adored him and they would troop around him after the services.

"Cookies for my little lambs, Christine," he would say after evensong, as they gathered in the sacristy. In church he presented a patriarchal picture, children stretching out their arms to him as he passed along the aisle. The boys who came for early communion once a month were treated to a beefsteak breakfast at the rectory. Dr. Houghton would go to the kitchen and announce: "Christine, I have twenty-eight of my boys. Have you got enough to eat?" Knowing his ways she would have baked bread the day before, and bought steak and vegetables at the Fulton Street Market. A huge pot of hominy would be cooking on the stove. It was no unusual thing for sixteen pounds of steak, with all manner of extras, to go down like grass before the mower's scythe, in the words of Dr. Houghton. The rectory was always gay with nephews and other small boys and girls who trotted about at the heels of "Uncle George." He would read them Brer Rabbit by the light of his candle, preferring this to the gaslight which was even then doomed to be snuffed out by the brighter glitter of electric light. There were strawberry festivals in the schoolroom in summer, and outings twice a month. Big wash baskets were filled with eatables for these affairs and, at Christmas and Thanksgiving, the room now used as the Guild Hall had long tables piled with parcels of food for the poor. Once a month throughout his ministry, Dr. Houghton rose at five o'clock in the morning and took train to Farmingdale to visit the orphans' home there.

In addition to his youthful following, the rector was continually besieged by a motley gathering of tramps and unfortunates begging for charity. He would march to the kitchen with a small army in rags and tatters at his heels, saying: "Here are my friends. Could you find them something to eat?" He slept with a basket of loose change beside his bed, so that none who asked for alms should go away empty-handed. Many a night when the city was sunk in sleep he threw his cassock over his night clothes and went down to the door, candle in hand, to admit a shivering *habitué* of the park benches. Their gratitude was not always genuine, and on at least two occasions Dr. Houghton was robbed, but he could never be persuaded that the men he had befriended had knowledge of the thefts. Once, all the silverware and valuables in the rectory were stolen. On the second occasion, thieves entered the church during the night and made off with five communion vessels, memorials studded with jewels.

He was quite fearless in his expeditions into gambling houses, dives and saloons, and was indifferent to personal danger or discomfort. On one occasion he was called on to visit a home where there was a case of malignant fever. He immediately said that he would be willing to go but that the case was in another parish and he might be intruding. He was told that the rector of the parish in question had declined to visit the sick man. "Then," said Dr. Houghton, "I will come." On his way home he stopped at his colleague's house and reported the visit. His own philosophy was very simple:

> I think nothing alien to me, nothing foreign to me,
> nothing void of interest to me, nothing a matter of un-
> concern to me, that has to do with my fellow man, with
> his weal or his woe. I, that am human, will never fail to be
> touched with a feeling for all human infirmity. I, that
> know the need of a never-failing charity, will never fail
> in the exercise of charity toward all men.

Tea, coffee, oatmeal and coal were freely dispensed to the poor, and clothing and medical care accompanied spiritual ministration at the church. Miss Marie Cortelyou Denslow, who lived across the street, had her office where the Lady Chapel now stands. She was a tiny figure with heavy ropes of hair and for many years she was the Lady of Charity at Transfiguration. She loved the parish with an abiding affection and, rain or shine, was always at her post. During the blizzard of 1888, Diee the chef, who by this time had married Christine and taken her away from the rectory, carried Miss Denslow across the street and over the snowdrifts so that she might give aid to those who needed it. She was as slight as a child and possessed of an indomitable spirit. Another of the faithful parishioners of this era was Mrs. Emily B. Hurry, who had sung in the original quartette.

One of Dr. Houghton's personal wards was an organist who had reached such a stage of drunkenness that all his friends and relatives had cast him off. For several months the rector took care of him on Saturday nights so that he might be fit to play on Sunday and not become a beggar. The organist was always very nervous during the services, however, and those close to him were continually on the alert to see that his music was on hand and the hymns were looked up in advance. Sometimes the organ blower would fall asleep during the sermon and the anxious reprobate would be in despair until a chorister rushed down to arouse the somnolent functionary. The congregation meanwhile would wait patiently for the music. In the same way a clergyman of brilliant talents and good family had become intemperate and was shunned as a disgrace to the cloth. Dr. Houghton took him in, furnished him with a room in the tower of the church, gave him a chance to reform and held on to him to the last. He would personally go to the Bowery to get him out of saloons when he had been sent downtown on an errand and had lingered on the way back.

The rectory was run along hospitable lines and a spare room on the first floor came to be known as the Cowley Room, for it stood in readiness to receive the Cowley priests on their visits to New York. Later on, the same hospitality was extended by Dr. Houghton to the members of the Order of the Holy Cross. There was strong feeling in the diocese against the monastic brotherhood when it was founded in 1881, but the rector of Transfiguration, always in sympathy with every phase of the Anglo-Catholic movement, gave it his support and to this day the friendliest relations exist between the church and Holy Cross.

The '80's dawned with a new step forward in the ecclesiastical history of Transfiguration. Celebration of the Daily Eucharist was introduced on October 3, 1880, and the surpliced choir filed into the church for the first time on the same date in the following year. The decade was one of major catastrophes and fortunes were made and lost overnight. The Wall Street panic of 1884 evoked scenes similar to the more recent *débâcle* of 1929. Four years later the great blizzard surprised New York, tying up transportation and inflicting memorable hardship on the poor. The East River was frozen over and firemen had to dig their horses out of the drifts to get to fires. By this time lower Fifth Avenue had passed its prime and the city's population had rolled up to 1,200,000. There was little traffic north of Columbus Circle, however, and the elevated trains went speeding up to Harlem past orchards and truck farms. An occasional suburbanite would drop off at Yorkville and stroll home by way of country lanes. Wild roses were picked by the wayside to adorn the handlebars of the tandem bicyclists who went scooting along the river on Sunday afternoons. The golf and tennis of modern youth had their forerunners in the skates and bicycles of the period. Fur tippets for frosty nights, winged hats and handsome whiskered escorts in toppers or tams, with whom to skate in Central Park, were the ambition of the chic damsel. Ginghams and dainty dimities, ribboned bonnets, mittens and balloon skirts, were tottering before an assault of high-necked shirt waists, gored skirts and shiny sailor hats, in the first embodiment of the tailored woman. The commentators of the day felt that femininity was in eclipse, as stenographers began to appear on the business horizon, bold girls who smacked the keys of their typewriters and essayed to storm a world of business men.

The masculine of the species, resplendent in pearl grey plugs, cassimeres, derbies or elegant straws settled on their pomaded heads, regarded this invasion with tolerance, but ill-concealed scepticism over the business capacity of a lady, if such she might be called once her hand had touched the grimy typewriter. Tidies, antimacassars, lambrequins and mother-of-pearl inlay were the fashion of the day, and homes were stuffy with horsehair. The Gerrys, Astors, Vanderbilts, Fishes and Bradley Martins were the hierarchy of the social world. While the Blue Danube was being played behind palms in many ballrooms, and the quadrilles, polkas, waltzes and Sir Roger de Coverley were being danced by the younger generation, Anthony Comstock and his evangelical brethren were denouncing from the pulpits the worldliness and increasing sinfulness of New York. The theatre was still the subject of bitter vituperation and, while the leading actors of the day flocked to The Little Church Around the Corner, their profession was constantly under attack in many of the other churches.

Although an admirer of Dr. Houghton, Dr. Talmage could never understand his kindliness to the theatrical profession. He was unremitting himself in his attacks on everything connected with the stage. But Broadway had another defender in the pulpit besides the rector of Transfiguration. Dr. Robert Collyer, known as the "blacksmith preacher," attended the more serious plays himself and regarded the stage with tolerance and a certain degree of sympathy. He was a striking figure, tall and bushy-haired, who strode through the streets with the gait of a backwoodsman. Both of the Tyngs had dropped out of the church life of New York by this time. The elder Dr. Tyng had resigned from St. George's in 1878, and his son had recently left Holy Trinity after holding his famous Premillennial Conference there. The Rev. Dr. W. R. Huntington was making himself popular at Grace Church as the successor to Dr. Potter, who had assumed the bishop's staff upon his uncle's death in 1887. The noonday services at old Trinity were drawing large crowds. The Rev. Phillips Brooks, Dean Frederic William Farrar and other contemporary clergymen of note, made this service a soothing hour in the business man's day. The financiers of the '80's, busy building up the fortunes that came to be fabulous in the public mind, left their trading and doffed their derbies to say a prayer in the quiet interior of Trinity.

IX

BOOTH'S LAST CURTAIN

MOST of Dr. Houghton's hopes for his parish had been realized by the '90's and his long ministry was now drawing to a close. His beard had grown white and his step was less steady as he walked down the aisle in the processional, for he was aging fast. By this time his church had international associations. The records were sprinkled with the names of visiting celebrities, and Henry Irving, Ellen Terry and Sarah Bernhardt had all attended services in the church while playing in New York. Miss Terry considered it one of the most charming places of worship she had ever been in. During the autumn of 1890 Dion Boucicault, that versatile Irishman who produced four hundred plays in his day, among them the popular *Colleen Bawn* and *Daddy O'Dowd*, was buried from The Little Church Around the Corner.

Three years later Edwin Booth died, and Dr. Houghton's church, with all its theatrical association and its historic possessions, made a singularly appropriate setting for his funeral. For years he had been a pew holder and a regular communicant. He was not one of the actors of whom Dr. Houghton was obliged to say, in remarking on their financial generosity: "A thousand, thousand times more gratifying would it be to have them come to church and drink the water of life and find rest for their souls." Booth had made a point of attending the services as often as he could and he had a genuine affection for the rector.

The reigning star of his generation was buried on a warm June day when the flowers were blooming lavishly in the *close* and half a dozen brides had already taken their wedding vows at the altar. In narrow-brimmed derbies and wide-brimmed straws, in swallow-tails and top hats, members of The

Players and most of the distinguished stage figures of the day filed in to the church. Booth's last gallery filled the street. Carriages lined the curb and policemen with grey helmets and bulging tail coats mounted guard at the entrance, as the crowd streamed inside for the funeral of the man who had long entertained them in the rôles of Iago, Hamlet, Richelieu and his other familiar characterizations.

The church was mellow now with the ripening of slow and harmonious growth. One by one, memorials had added to its intrinsic grace. Dr. Houghton was never tired of contemplating the lustrous interior, the friendly pews and the shadowy alcoves. The church was alive to him, a volume of sermons in which he constantly dipped. The long aisles and the low, dark ceiling suggested depth and repose. The figures of saints and prophets in stone and stained glass spread benediction over the nave. To the very end he worked for the perfection of his church. Few clergymen have centred their lives so completely around their parishes as he, and the reputation of Transfiguration was inseparable from his own personality. Night and day he encountered strong currents of life in a setting of cloistered calm. No sign of the tragedies and violence that brushed his daily path obtruded on the serenity of his church. He believed in the last word in form, in "sacred pictures and memorial windows, lights and flowers, colours to mark the changing seasons, garments of beauty and holiness, the white-robed choristers and the Processional Cross." He demanded the utmost literacy of service, insisting that "whatever is read or sung in the House of God be read or sung in a manner befitting the place."

Brides in the elaborate attire of the '90's passed to and fro on the garden path, arriving in such numbers now that Dr. Houghton set 10 o'clock at night as the deadline for tying the nuptial knot. On sunny days, when jonquils and tulips bloomed at the church door and the fountain sprayed its sparkling shower of crystal, Dr. Houghton sat in his high, stiff chair under the shade of the elms and remembered forty years ago when the doors of his chapel first opened on a rural scene. The seasons flitted fast with his declining years. The tulips withered on their stalks and the full-blown roses of June scented the *close*. The leaves whirled scarlet and yellow at the church door and snow powdered the ashen branches of winter. Each passing month brought added content to the rectory, for Dr. Houghton had now been promised the parish house and the lich-gate, both of which he had desired for many years. Soon after Booth was buried, Mrs. Sarah Jane Zabriskie, whose family lived on the next street to the church, and who had long been a devoted parishioner, gave $70,000, which was blessed on the altar and used to buy the house adjoining the church on the east. In another year the surpliced choir, the guilds and the various societies of the parish were provided with some of the accommodation that they had long needed.

"Will not Transfiguration be lovely when all is done as is now proposed?" Dr. Houghton exclaimed in momentary enthusiasm for his beloved edifice. "Please God, let me live to see all done and paid for." But because of his widespread charity there was a shortage of cash in the church treasury at this time. Taking his parishioners mildly to task one Sunday morning he gave them a reproachful talk on their neglect:

> We can go to the country and deny ourselves no manner of thing that is good; we have our yachts and carriages, and horses and dogs; subscribe to our oratorios; go to matinées; have fine dinners and entertainments; fine luncheons at Delmonico's; belong to this club and that club—pay our dues like men; smoke the best and costliest of cigars; drink the choicest of champagnes and burgundies; wear our diamonds and rings, and laces and silks; fill the air around us with our high-priced perfumes; live at hotels and in luxurious apartments; and do our only retrenching in the things that pertain to God and His Church.

An actor who happened to hear his sermon wrote to the *Dramatic News* and immediately an editorial was printed pointing out that the theatrical and musical professions were especially the care of the rector of The Little Church

Around the Corner, and that his "confessionals were not recorded in the newspapers but by the angels, since he heard the confessions of more sinners and worse sinners than any priest in New York, outside of the Roman Catholic Church." There was an instant response from the people of the stage. Mrs. Catherine Holland, widow of the actor who had brought the church much of its fame, sent $250 on behalf of herself and her three sons, and contributions came in from all parts of the country, until the required amount was greatly exceeded. Dr. Houghton was embarrassed. He had not intended to expose the financial cracks in his church. However, he accepted the money in the spirit in which it was given and blessed it on the altar. He had avoided mentioning his own plight but, as a matter of fact, his salary was $9,500 in arrears and the treasurer, Charles N. Kent, wrote to him: "Surely never did one ever give so much in love and affection, prayers and good counsel to a parish as you have given and are still giving at Transfiguration. It is something that money can never repay."

The vestry finally insisted on selling to St. Stephen's Parish the chapel on Sixty-ninth Street which Dr. Houghton had built in 1876 in the image of Transfiguration. Its pews were free and it was really the embodiment of his original idea for his own church, a place of worship that would be without owners of "little pens." It was built in the same haphazard manner as the mother church, with a low ceiling and odd nooks and corners. Its grounds were laid out with trees and shrubs. The Rev. Edward C. Houghton, one of "Uncle George's" nephews, was rector. But the chapel did not flourish and reluctantly Dr. Houghton consented at last to its sale.

The new chancel of The Little Church Around the Corner was opened and used for the first time in the winter of 1895 and a few months later a modern organ was installed to take the place of the old one. Thus, Dr. Houghton lived to see his parish with a completed church, an endowment fund of $150,000, a free library and all the guilds and societies equipped for perpetuation. And at last, as his life ebbed to a close, his fondest wish was fulfilled—the lich-gate. It was given by Mrs. Franklin Delano, the former Miss

Laura Astor, who had been coming to the church since her girlhood days. The Stations of the Cross and the old Spanish, Italian and French paintings that give the transept the air of an art gallery were also her gift, chosen from her own private collection.

The gate, now one of the distinguishing marks of the church, was finished in the spring of 1896. It carried out in the most minute detail the rector's longing for a niche for the wayfarer at his hospitable entrance. "Forty-and-six years was this temple in building!" he exclaimed in thankfulness when at last it was finished as the crowning touch to his parish. To this day the gate presents great interest to the passerby and to those who walk through it on their way to the church. The copper nubbling of the slanting roof is weathered with the grey-green of verdigris. Under the shady canopy is a marble statue of the Lord, set on a pedestal and enclosed by a small railing. At the base is carved the inscription: *Come unto Me and I will refresh you.* The silhouetted figure may be seen from all sides against a background of shrubs, like some wayside shrine in Europe. To the left is a stone drinking fountain with the words: *Whosoever drinketh of the water which I will give shall never thirst.* At the other side is a desk for a Bible and prayer book.

There are only three lich-gates in this country. One is in the diocese of Maine, and the other is at the entrance to St. Clement's Church, St. Paul, Minn. There are a few in England and Wales, but the one which most closely resembles in style and structure the lich-gate at Transfiguration is to be found at Clifton-Hampden in Oxfordshire. Few of the mediæval gates survive, as they were made of wood and decayed in course of time, but there is an ancient one at Bray, Berkshire, dating back to 1448. Another interesting lich-gate is to be found at Berrynarbor, Devon, and there are no less than three in a churchyard at Troutbeck, Westmoreland, one in the shape of a cross.

The original use of the lich-gate is of such antiquity that it has almost been forgotten. The name comes from the old Anglo-Saxon "lich," a corpse, and the root is found in lichwake, a watch over the dead, lichway, a path

imp RLB   RL Boyer

THE CHRIST OF THE LICH GATE

by which the dead are borne in, and lichfield, the field of the dead. Its early function was simply to provide a roof or canopy at the churchyard entrance, under which the pallbearers might rest the coffin and await the coming of the priest. After the introductory part of the burial office was read, the procession formed and the body was borne inside. In its primitive state it was usually a thatched or tiled porch, or else a simple shed of wood. Sometimes it was built of stone. Later it became more elaborate and was used as a little outdoor chapel. Strangely mediæval in its skyscraper setting, the lich-gate with its pagoda roof is the first glimpse the visitor gets of The Little Church Around the Corner.

Dr. Houghton lived to see it completed and his eyes feasted on it with abiding satisfaction, but he died before it was consecrated. Nor did he live to celebrate the fiftieth anniversary of the church, much as he had hoped to round out his half century as rector. He died on November 17, 1897, just as the shades of evening closed in on the bedroom screened by one of the elms that his friend, Mr. de Peyster, had planted many years before. His nephew had come to assist him fifteen days earlier, but Dr. Houghton had denied all intention of relinquishing his duties. "I shall remain in my place unto the end," he had announced with great determination. But from the moment that some of the responsibility slid from his shoulders he began to fail. He attended Holy Communion on the day of his death and read matins at nine. He had gone out in the rain on one of his errands of mercy a few days before and had caught cold. While evensong was being read he was in his bedroom, drawing painful breaths. His niece sent for the Rev. Edmund B. Smith, the curate, and he entered the room reading the service for the dying. Only a few months earlier the aged rector had said:

> What a privileged parish has this of the Transfiguration been in ministering the last things at the last to those who sought them only at the last! What a record of last words, last prayers, last sacraments, last absolvings and last blessings!

He had ministered to the dying under all conditions, the gambler who had been stabbed, the repentant magdalen, the fever-stricken child, the sinner and the saint. It was now his own turn. But the light had already failed for Dr. Houghton; his lips could barely frame the responses, and he died an hour and a half after he had fallen ill. Thousands passed by the bier of the beloved rector of The Little Church Around the Corner, prayers and tears mingling in sincere tribute to a saintly figure. From nightfall to dawn the Sisters of St. Mary, bowed forms in black, kept vigil beside the fitful candles. Negroes shuffled past with awed faces, and the women of the neighbourhood, whom he had made his particular care, dabbed at their eyes and mumbled the words of an unfamiliar prayer. Policemen, postmen, street sweepers and various night workers dropped in to the church between their rounds. The humble ones to whom he had extended his charity, the tramps and unfortunates who had found him always ready to aid them, hovered around the iron fence. Admission for the funeral service was by ticket only, but hundreds gathered in the street and waited for the coffin to be borne through the lich-gate. A black pall lay over it, embroidered by the members of St. Anna's Guild with the prayer he had asked them to offer when he passed on "to the country that lies beyond the seas and the sunset." It was simply: *Grant him, Lord, eternal rest: and let light perpetual shine upon him*. Bishop Potter read the burial office. Ten dioceses were represented and there were delegations from The Players, The Lambs, the Twelfth Night Club, the Actors' Fund, the Elks and the Actors' National Protective Union. Church and stage walked side by side at the bier of Dr. Houghton, who had worked for thirty years to bring them together.

The founder died at a time when the New York he had known was about to undergo a sweeping change from the violet-tinted age of romance to the realities of science. The Victorian era was drawing to a close, and the storms that had rent the Episcopal Church had tapered off to a suave acceptance of High and Low Church elements on both sides of the Atlantic. The '90's was a decade that combined reforming zeal in the pulpits with great social brilliance. Dr. Parkhurst, preaching in Madison Square Church, had denounced the New York City administration and had investigated the Tenderloin to prove his charges. In 1893 his home was besieged by women who had been driven out of a raided resort and who blamed him for their eviction. He took as many of them as he could into his home and fed them. He was a much discussed figure in these days as he walked in Inverness cape and derby to the Lexow Committee hearings, with a bearded and moustached guard at his heels. He carried his campaign to such an effective conclusion that Tammany was defeated and Theodore Roosevelt was appointed Police Commissioner of New York.

In the year of Dr. Houghton's death, Mrs. Astor moved uptown to Sixty fifth Street. Four years earlier the other Astor house at Thirty-fourth Street had been torn down and the Waldorf-Astoria had been built on the site. Oscar speedily became a favourite and wrested some of its prestige from the house of Delmonico. Soon the residential tide, which had remained inviolate heretofore below Forty-second Street, swept uptown, clearing the way for an invasion of trade. Presently a row of mansions was built on upper Fifth Avenue where shanties, trees and green fields had been the sole outlook when Dr. Houghton founded his parish. The population of the city was now about 1,500,000. The trolley was running the old horse-car off the streets, and local pride in the incandescent light led to festive neighbourhood outings in streetcars strung with coloured lights. The hansom was still gliding about in dignified aloofness, but the era of automobiles and aeroplanes was on its way. Sunday buggy rides were out of fashion.

The Bradley Martin ball at the Waldorf in 1897, with its gorgeous historical pageant, and footmen in pale blue and gold opening carriage doors, had evoked the criticism of the clergy, notably Dr. William S. Rainsford, the six-foot-two occupant of the pulpit of St. George's, who considered the function an orgy of extravagance. International weddings were in vogue. The fashion set by Miss Jennie Jerome, when she married Lord Randolph Churchill in the '70's, gathered impetus toward the close of the Victorian era, with the elaborate wedding in Grace Church of sixteen-year-old Cornelia Martin and the Earl of Craven, followed by the Vanderbilt-Marlborough, Castellane-Gould and other international alliances. Divorce was becoming a vexed topic in Episcopalian circles.

The Easter parade which swept up and down Fifth Avenue had the *cachet* of Ward McAllister and was more than ever one of the sights of the metropolis, with its rustling silks, waxed moustaches and cart-wheel hats. Bustles were waning but leg-o'-mutton sleeves billowed out with regal splendour. The well-dressed churchgoer favoured a huge Ascot with perhaps a diamond horseshoe. Silk vests, high collars and stiff bosoms were still *au fait*, although an occasional covert coat was cutting in on the historic Prince Albert on Sunday mornings. Trade still dawdled below Twenty-eighth Street and well away from Fifth Avenue. Brownstone stoops extended all the way from Washington Square to Central Park, and there were brilliant splashes of colour where flowers and grass lent a leisurely note to the sophisticated thoroughfare. In spring the tulips nodded their scarlet and yellow bells and the stiff geraniums stood like scarlet-coated soldiers beside the shrinking fuschias that drooped in magenta confusion along the pavements of Fifth Avenue.

X

A NEW RECTOR AND AN OLD TRADITION

THE Houghton tradition was carried on without a break when the second rector took up the work of the parish. The church maintained its quiet policy of service at all hours. Both of the Houghtons believed that a rector should always be accessible, and the younger man ministered the trust left by his uncle in such a manner that The Little Church Around the Corner continued to be synonymous with kindliness and benevolent assistance. The Rev. Dr. George Clarke Houghton began his work as vicar of the parish on November 2, 1897, only a few days before the founder died. He had been persuaded by his uncle to study for the ministry and, in urging him to accept the call to Transfiguration, the old man had said: "Only you can give me the needed assistance in carrying on my work." He was already a thoroughly experienced priest, who had expanded a small Hoboken parish into a flourishing incumbency.

The second Dr. Houghton was born in New York on December 17, 1852, the son of Frederick and Anna Houghton. He attended the parish school in the early days of Transfiguration, along with his cousin Edward. Both boys were persuaded by "Uncle George" that the church was the proper sphere for their talents. The younger George spent so much of his time at the rectory in his boyhood days that Transfiguration was a second home to him. He was graduated in 1867 from St. Stephen's College, Annandale, and then entered the General Theological Seminary, that cluster of buildings in Chelsea Village where so many of the divines of the last century received their theological training. He was ordained in St. Marks-in-the-Bouwerie by Bishop Potter and served for a time as curate at Trinity Church. Later he was transferred to Saint Chrysostom's Chapel, also in Trinity parish. After being there for eight years he became rector of Trinity Church, Hoboken, where he remained for eighteen years until called to his uncle's church. Dr. Houghton freed Trinity Church from debt, enlarged it and enriched it with gifts, among them a reredos purchased by contributions from the couples he had married, for before he ever came to The Little Church Around the Corner he had had wide experience in solemnizing marriages. He built a church of rough boulders and timbers at Pine Hill in the Catskills, where he spent his holidays. He and a vestryman did most of the physical labour themselves, heaving stone and hauling logs. And when his rough-hewn house of worship was finished, it was named after the church that his uncle had built in New York. During this period he preached many of the baccalaureate sermons at the Stevens Institute, and the graduates in after years recalled long evenings at the ivy-covered rectory in Hoboken, where Dr. Houghton told ghost stories over a flickering fire.

Back in the '70's Dr. Houghton had married a girl whose voice, singing a love ballad to the accompaniment of a spinet, had floated through a window as he went visiting with his uncle in Old Chelsea. He was entranced, and later, when he met Miss Mary Creemer Pirsson, a beauty with skin of magnolia texture, a cleft in her chin and eyes of gentian blue, he fell deeply in love with her. She was the daughter of one of his uncle's friends, Talbot Pirsson, and before long they were married. Their romance was a genuine idyll that lasted for thirty years. When he first met Mary, young Houghton was a serious-faced youth with a Roman nose, a fringe of dark, curling hair and side-burns. As years went on, like most of his contemporaries, he abandoned his whiskers and became clean shaven. Later in life he put on weight and was a portly figure in his declining years.

The rectory had new and enhanced charm when Dr. Houghton moved in with his wife and daughter, Mary Gertrude Houghton. Mrs. Houghton continued to sing her ballads, to browse through old book shops—a taste she had in common with her husband—and to pounce on the running installments of the serials of that day. *Robert Elsmere* was creating a stir in ecclesiastical circles and Kipling and Stevenson were being published in *Scribner's* and *The Century*. Mark Twain was in high favour and, at the other end of the scale, were the Elsie books, best sellers of their day. Both of the Houghtons were insatiable readers, the rector leaning to detective tales and ghost stories, Mrs. Houghton to romance and the poets. Although not much of a theatregoer, the new rector pursued the policy of his uncle in every respect with regard to the stage. He deplored the censorious denunciation of the theatrical profession that was common in many pulpits. Society had been won over, but it was not until the close of the century that the churches began to regard the theatre with tolerance, let alone approval. For years actors had been tabooed by the church as sinful creatures, but a change in the tone of the drama and an infusion of the morality theme had converted a number of churchmen to the idea that the stage might have ethical values. The broader-minded were able to detect an occasional text lurking in the current fare.

These were dazzling days on Broadway. The problem and society plays were at their height. The works of Pinero, Wilde and Henry Arthur Jones were in vogue. *Lady Windermere's Fan* and *Trelawney of the Wells* were two of the current hits. Richard Mansfield, a regular communicant at The Little Church Around the Corner, was giving Broadway a taste of George Bernard Shaw with *Arms and the Man* at the Herald Square Theatre. The Floradora Sextette, and Edna May as the Belle of New York, were the toasts of the day. The Gibson girl was coming into fashion and the Trilby craze was on. The matinée idols were having their innings, and the classic profiles of Robert C. Hilliard, Robert Mantell, James K. Hackett, John Drew, William Faversham, Walter Hampden, De Wolf Hopper, Kyrle Bellew and William Collier, to mention only a few, evoked many sighs across the footlights.

Their feminine colleagues were also basking in high favour. Maude Adams, Ada Rehan, Mrs. Minnie Maddern Fiske, Fanny Davenport, Mrs.

Thomas Whiffen, Kate Claxton, Clara Morris and Mary Anderson were all delighting Broadway. Lillian Russell was playing at the Casino, and Ethel Barrymore's rich contralto was just beginning to be heard across the footlights. The Empire Theatre, which had opened with stock under Charles Frohman's auspices, was the last word in gilded and plush magnificence. Vaudeville was in its heyday at Tony Pastor's, the London Theatre and Harry Miner's Bowery. Koster and Bial's was patronized by the bloods of the day, and moving pictures were a mere whisper in the future. The Metropolitan Opera and the Horse Show were at the peak of their splendour.

On a June day in 1898, five years after Booth's death, Jefferson unveiled John La Farge's memorial to the great Thespian. The ceremony was at evensong, with William Bispham, Stanford White and Richard Watson Gilder standing beside Jefferson as he drew the curtain from the memorial, the gift of The Players. The window dominates the transept, a mediæval histrionic student sitting with a mask in his hands which he has just removed from his face. His gaze is on the mask and below is the inscription:

> "As one, in suffering all, that suffers nothing;
> A man that fortune's buffets and rewards
> Has ta'en with equal thanks."
> *Hamlet III, 2.*

Booth had once told a friend that this was his chosen epitaph—words that he had repeated countless times as Hamlet. The memorial inscription in stained glass reads: *To the glory of God, and in loving memory of Edwin Booth. This Window has been placed here by The Players.* The Bible on the lectern was also the gift of The Players in memory of Booth, who founded the club. Jefferson, who had "christened" The Little Church Around the Corner, was now well on in years. He retired from the stage six years later and died at Palm Beach in 1906. He was buried at Buzzard's Bay, where he had always spent his summers.

The parish was now bustling with activity. Its reputation for hospitality continued to attract an extraordinary following of one kind and another. Fifty and sixty letters begging food or aid for the sick would reach the rectory in a day. Dr. Houghton believed in self-help and put a mild curb on indiscriminate charity. St. Martin's Guild was established to supply the poor with clothing at a nominal price. His stated reason for setting a small fee was that the "Christian religion ought not to aid in pauperizing, but is bound to inculcate self-respect and self-support among all classes of people." His Coal Club was another practical charity, designed to remove the necessity for the poor buying coal by the scuttleful and thereby paying exorbitant prices for it. Saint Persis Guild was an early employment bureau for those out of work. All of the guilds were designed to inspire self-help and give the needy the support they required. The soft-heartedness of the first Dr. Houghton had brought many beggars around who had sponged continually on his charity, and his nephew took a firm stand where shiftless tramps came whining at the door. Yet the needy poor were abundantly aided at Transfiguration. Dr. Houghton frequently made personal deliveries in hansoms and, later on, in his motor car, leaving groceries and medicine at tenement homes.

One of his innovations was a church paper in which he published many whimsies and thoughts of his own. *The Kalendar* made its first appearance in February, 1900, a four-page leaflet. On the front page was the order of music for the ensuing Sunday. The other three pages were used for short talks on church matters and for mild admonitions to those who did not come to church on Sunday. Fifteen hundred copies of *The Kalendar* were printed and distributed each week. They reflect what was going on in the church at that time and contain occasional sidelights such as this:

> The beautiful ice-crystals about our churchyard fountain during the cold days of the past two weeks have received favourable criticism. They are not entirely due to nature's work. "John" has a hand in their construction and so regulates the flow of water as to produce artistic results.

Dr. Houghton took this means of making known his needs and desires to his congregation. The characters Edgar and Thomas, Dorothy and Melinda, Clarence and Walter, chatted back and forth, discussing parish affairs and reflecting the thoughts of the rector. In *The Kalendar* Dr. Houghton continually referred to his desire for a bell. At last, through the offerings of his parishioners, the twelve-hundred-pound bell, which still peals for the consecration at Holy Communion, was placed in the tower. Like his uncle, he paid many visits to the Negroes, who were still attached to the church. The last of the old coloured retainers passed on with the close of the century. When the church was built, a number of New Yorkers owned Negro slaves and, even after the Civil War, the tradition persisted in certain homes. When the second Dr. Houghton took over the parish, Commodore Gerry still had a former slave named William Wood in his household. Servants were becoming less numerous as science and invention invaded the home. Steam heat and electric light had simplified domestic arrangements and freed the ancient taper from its honorary function as feeder to the round, white globes of the gas-lit age. The city was still small enough for people to know one another on the same block and give friendly greetings in passing, but the millionaires who had amassed their fortunes in the '90's were now building their homes across from Central Park, and trade was invading lower Fifth Avenue. The first of the apartment houses had begun to rise above the old four-storey level, precursors of the skyscraper age.

As the murmur of commerce grew to a roar, the *close* of Transfiguration became more remarkable for its tranquillity, and many tarried at the lichgate in passing. The foliage was thicker and the garden more verdant with each passing year. Dust and gasolene had not yet stifled the budding shoots, and carriages rolled smoothly past on streets of asphalt. Women in toques of violets, with sealskin jackets, small round muffs and veils framing delicate features, lingered to pray in the iridescence of the church. Mrs. Houghton watched the endless stream of brides with all the interest of a newcomer at the rectory. She would slip into the church now and again and sit in a back

THE REVEREND DOCTOR GEORGE CLARKE HOUGHTON
SECOND RECTOR

pew while a wedding ceremony was in progress. On the last day of April, 1902, she died, and a shadow fell on the rectory that was never wholly removed in the lifetime of the second rector of Transfiguration. He mourned her silently and constantly with a grief that did not diminish with the years. Dr. Houghton filled the rectory with photographs of his wife, so that his eye could rest on her countenance whichever way he turned. He did his parish desk work at night and read detective stories till the coming of dawn. His study light shone like an unquenchable cruse, perpetuating the old tradition that the rector was always ready for the coming of those who needed the sacraments of the church.

Mrs. Houghton was buried in Kensico Cemetery, where her husband had a white granite mausoleum built for her. She died on a Wednesday, and every Wednesday morning for seventeen years he went to her resting place after early communion with a bouquet of flowers. A requiem mass was celebrated at Transfiguration each year on her birthday, May 11. He lavished some of his affection by devising St. Mary's Chapel in her memory, a memorial of marble and mosaic. Hour after hour he knelt and prayed under the ruby flame in the tiny sanctuary familiarly known as the Lady Chapel. On the brass credence is the inscription in Latin: "Without ceasing I make mention of you in my prayers." It was consecrated four years after his wife died but as long as he lived Dr. Houghton worked to perfect its detail. The chapel is pure Gothic, a dark and pointed setting for its shrine of lyric loveliness, an altar of snowy marble seamed with blue and gold mosaic. The *motif* of the carving on the altar and reredos is the grape vine and sheaf of wheat. Eight Gothic columns support the table, and a small cross of onyx flashes in the tabernacle door. *The Last Supper* is reproduced in cobalt and gold mosaic, and the floor is patterned with marble mosaic. The ceiling is of antique oak and a coppery light streams through panels of leaded glass. The centre window shows the perspective of the east end of the church and the high altar, a unique effect in stained glass. Six wrought iron doors, separating the Lady Chapel from the brides' chapel, represent in twelve miniatures the life of St.

Mary, stained glass copies of old Italian masters. All of the careful detail was conceived by Dr. Houghton, who succeeded in creating a memorial of rare and fragile beauty for his wife. He kept it as a shrine, apart from the activities of the church. But an exception was made when Miss Denslow died in November, 1907. She was laid in state in the Lady Chapel, the site of the office where she had dispensed charity for many years. Dr. Houghton's daughter was married in the same month to the Rev. Charles Strombom, a curate of the church.

XI

LOVE, HONOUR AND OBEY

THE path leading from the lich-gate to the church was now perpetually strewn with confetti, and the little green door of Dr. Houghton's office swung to and fro on youth that was beginning to be more casual in its approach to the wedding ceremony. The business girl with her independent ways had stolen a march on parental supervision and was no longer bound by apron strings. Dr. Houghton did what he could to stem the steady stream of candidates but, as rector of The Little Church Around the Corner, he could not escape his destiny, and in later life he came to be known as the "marrying parson." He preferred not to have the figures counted but during his incumbency he performed at least 30,000 wedding ceremonies, and his admonitions are still remembered in many parts of the world.

Getting married at Transfiguration was no easy or informal matter, yet girls and youths came flocking through the lich-gate as if it were simple to take their wedding vows at Dr. Houghton's altar. The old-world atmosphere of the church, with its fragrant and leaf-swept *close*, drew brides from far and near, and the fame of its theatrical weddings gave it a certain piquancy in the public mind. It was considered charming and unconventional to be married at The Little Church Around the Corner, and Dr. Houghton's insistence on canonical rules failed utterly to discourage applicants. It was not unusual for girls to come from distant parts of the country, saying that they had once seen the church and had made up their minds that they would be married nowhere else. It is a matter of history that one girl came from Switzerland and another from the Argentine for the express purpose of being married there, and American babies have been hurried home from Rome and the

Philippines for baptism in the Chapel of the Holy Family, because their mothers were brides of The Little Church Around the Corner. This is part of the chain of sentiment that links its brides with the church, wherever they go in after life.

The loss of his wife had made Dr. Houghton doubly sympathetic to the young people who sought his ministration. After each ceremony he would put his arm around the bridegroom's shoulder and say: "Be kind to her." Then he would turn to the bride and say: "Take good care of him." Now and again he would urge them both "to be good mates." Kindness had been his wife's injunction to all those who had come to her for advice and counsel. On his golden jubilee he looked back over this stretch of years and said:

> One of my pleasantest and most satisfactory recollections is that I have started so many men and women on the road to two of the greatest and most normal of human experiences—marriage and parenthood. I like to believe that most of the marriages I have performed, if not all, have turned out happily.

He was forced to put a curb on weddings, however, for the impression had spread, because of the kindliness of his uncle, that the church was a Gretna Green where marriage was easy and informal. Even more of a ritualist than the founder, he did all he could to disabuse people of this idea. He discouraged hasty unions and, during the war, was not inclined to marry the young soldiers who dropped in with prospective brides. Miss Mary C. Hanlon, the competent assistant who has smoothed the way for hundreds of brides at The Little Church Around the Corner, and has aided many flustered bridegrooms in their hunt for missing rings, would plead the cause of the soldier candidates until Dr. Houghton, if fully persuaded of their sincerity, would at last give in with the observation: "I am swayed by my sentimental secretary."

It has been estimated that Dr. Houghton turned away 20,000 couples during his ministry, because they did not meet the strict requirements he imposed. It was not at all unusual for him to refuse the marriage ceremony to a hundred couples a month. There was no use attempting subterfuge or deceit with this perspicacious churchman, for he was thoroughgoing by nature and would spend hours getting to the bottom of their stories. He was profoundly experienced in this sphere and was able sometimes to shake the conviction of confident youth embarking blindly on a doubtful course. It was easier to come under his influence than to break away, for Dr. Houghton's sense of moral responsibility extended beyond his own immediate functions as a priest asked to solemnize a wedding. If he thought the applicants were likely to seek the offices of the church elsewhere, he would devote himself to persuading them to take time and consider what they were doing. Delay was his advice for all dubious cases. He was well aware that, once outside the lichgate, they could find a way to get married, but to his dying day he sought to preserve the marriage tie according to his lights as a strict churchman.

There were many reasons why he should make the barriers steep. Strangers in town, looking for a suitable church in which to be married, were invariably directed by cabmen to The Little Church Around the Corner. Hacks would arrive with couples who had met at sea or abroad, and the old tradition of tolerance at Transfiguration wiped out sectarian differences. It was not unusual for vows to be taken in foreign languages. At the same time, the proximity of the parish to the restaurants and theatres during the early part of the century, brought applicants late at night who had dined well and were feeling merry. Dr. Houghton invariably refused to perform the ceremony under those circumstances but would tell the pair to come back on the following day, when he would consider their applications. No roisterers found a haven in his church. Now and again a prospective bridegroom left the rectory in high dudgeon after creating a scene because the rector had refused the sacrament of marriage.

Divorces were just beginning to be common and all the churches were deeply concerned over this new social problem. Bishop Potter, immensely popular and a liberal like his uncle, was unbending on the subject, for, while other denominations were beginning to relax a little, the Episcopal Church held firm to its canons. Dr. Houghton personally believed that there was no such thing as divorce and that marriage ended only with death. Thus, divorce was an insuperable barrier at The Little Church Around the Corner during his ministry, just as it is to-day, and in the last thirty years a surprising number of stage stars have found themselves ineligible for marriage at its hospitable altar. Dr. Houghton considered secrecy almost as much of an obstacle to marriage as divorce. He refused to solemnize a runaway marriage, a secret marriage or any union that seemed to him to be palpably unsuitable. A girl was obliged to tell her mother of her intention, even though the announcement entailed a scene, as it often did in cases of this kind. He would insist on a telegram or message being sent to relatives before he would proceed with the ceremony, and he thought nothing of waiting hours for the young people to make up their minds on taking this step. The third requirement of the church was baptism. A searching questionnaire was filled out and the applicants were referred to specific definitions:

> *Before marriage every man is a bachelor; no man is a widower until after wife's burial. Before marriage every woman is spinster; no woman is widow until after husband's burial.*

The preliminaries did not end there. Many who had arrived in a flippant spirit paused and gave thought when told to place their hands on the Bible and repeat:

> *We, the undersigned, in the presence of God, hereby solemnly declare, without reservation or evasion, that the above facts, and all other statements, whether in writing or given orally, are true in every particular to the best of our knowledge and belief. We are of legal age and there is absolutely no impediment, opposition or objection to our marriage.*

Dr. Houghton succeeded in making this oath so impressive that candidates sometimes broke down and confessed that they were covering up impediments and would like to make a clean breast of their deceit. As a rule, they acknowledged that they were keeping their wedding secret or were runaways. Since it was Dr. Houghton's publicly expressed opinion that hasty marriages were the fastest route to the divorce court, he took infinite pains with couples of this sort, and toward the end of his ministry he revealed that he had persuaded more than three thousand runaway couples to go home and obtain their parents' consent, or else postpone the ceremony until it was regarded in a more favourable light by their elders. There were strange scenes in the study as Dr. Houghton threshed things out with strong-headed youngsters who thought him an old fogey for being so unbending with them. The prospective brides tried blandishments, tears and coercion, without making the least impression on his resolve to swing them his way or else deny them the offices of his church. They would even get down on their knees and beg for his sympathy at times. He was proof against arguments and tears, but his daughter knew best how those scenes wore on his nerves. Levity was frowned on severely by the "marrying parson," and he impressed on many heedless couples the etiquette of approaching the solemnization of their marriage vows in a reverent manner.

In order further to discourage hasty marriages, Dr. Houghton announced in the autumn of 1907 that he would begin publishing banns from the pulpit. This caused quite a sensation in the church, as it marked the revival of a custom abandoned in the United States although still canonical law. To this day Dr. Ray posts the banns for about fifty per cent of the weddings in his church. Until "obey" was officially dropped from the marriage ceremony Dr. Houghton insisted on its use even when brides were first winning emancipation from this declaration. One story is told of his determination to make a bride conform, even against her will. A large and fashionable wedding was being solemnized before the high altar. A curate had conducted the rehearsal; otherwise the *contretemps* would probably never have arisen. The church was packed with relatives and friends. The ceremony was going smoothly until Dr. Houghton reached the words—"and to obey."

"I don't want to say that," whispered the bride.

Dr. Houghton looked at her and waited.

"She doesn't want to say 'obey,' " murmured the bridegroom.

"And to obey," came Dr. Houghton's voice, insistent this time.

Quaveringly the bride responded: "And to obey."

The social structure was changing fast at this time, and New York was becoming a high-paced city of business and commerce. The Flatiron Building was presaging the tall skyline and Chauncey M. Depew was at the height of his form as a *raconteur*. Dinner was eaten in a leisurely manner and men lounged at the bars on their way home from business. The social nucleus moulded by Ward McAllister was beginning to lose its form, as the population grew larger and more cosmopolitan. Wright had made his first aeroplane flight and electric lights flashed with increasing magnitude on Broadway. Formal calls and courteous notes diminished in favour as the telephone and telegraph became commonplace utilities. Americans were beginning to travel, and going to Europe was no longer like a Polar expedition. The brownstone fronts and their striped awnings were standing pat in face of an irresistible tide of destruction, but the motor car was chasing old Dobbin off the streets. Smart turn-outs still came spanking up to The Little Church Around the Corner, however, and coachmen looked down their noses at the automobiles that drew up with shining arrogance at the lich-gate. The city was moving fast, but the problems brought to the Episcopal confessional varied little. Broken hearts were still patched up and wedding vows said in the church that aged as New York grew big and lusty. The churches were packed, although it was feared that motoring was going to prove a great distraction—worse, in fact, than the demon bicycle which was now fading into the background. Pulpit crusading was no longer a popular Sunday pastime. Clergymen deplored divorce and exhorted their feminine parishioners to eschew the ungraceful and unrefined game of tennis which offended against all the canons of womanly dignity and delicacy. Croquet was still considered the thing for garden parties, but the women's colleges were beginning to show alarming signs of emancipation, with pompadoured flappers bounding around the tennis courts in stiffly starched shirt waists, their long, black skirts flapping at their heels as they leaped in the air. Flaming Youth's own ancestors! Homes, as well as costumes, were due for a great simplification with the dawn of the Edwardian era, and plush was soon to follow horsehair to the attic.

XII

O. HENRY'S ENVOI

A LONELY figure with a keen eye and a photographic mind was prowling about in the neighbourhood of The Little Church Around the Corner as the twentieth century progressed. He lived at the Caledonia on West Twenty-sixth Street, and in his strolls around Madison Square and farther north, he grew familiar with the changing moods of the church. Its snow-burdened eaves and lowly towers were ample provocation for O. Henry, whose cabbies, hoboes, shop-girls, "princes and queens clad in all the silks and gems of the world," haunted the vicinity of the church as "Manhattan, the night-blooming cereus, was beginning to unfold its dead-white, heavy-odoured petals."

The outlines of the church can be detected in several of O. Henry's tales and in at least one he mentions it specifically by name. In *The Romance of a Busy Broker* he winds up: "Don't you remember, Harvey? We were married last evening at 8 o'clock in The Little Church Around the Corner." In his preoccupation with ticker tape the busy broker had forgotten that his secretary was now his wife. But, in *The Cop and the Anthem*, O. Henry describes the church in its relation to Soapy:

> On his bench in Madison Square Soapy moved uneasily. A dead leaf fell in Soapy's lap. That was Jack Frost's calling card. Soapy craved for three months on the Island, the nice comfortable Blackwell's Island where the benches wouldn't be so cold and hard.

But try as he would Soapy could not get himself arrested. He had a sumptuous meal and did not pay for it. He heaved a stone through a window but no one took any notice. He stole an umbrella and he flirted openly with a girl, but all to no avail. Soapy was doomed to liberty. Then he abandoned misdeeds and clung to an iron fence. For on an "unusually quiet corner" he had come to a standstill:

> Here was an old church, quaint and rambling and gabled. Through one violet-stained window a soft light glowed, where, no doubt, the organist loitered over the keys, making sure of his mastery of the coming Sabbath anthem. For there drifted out to Soapy's ears sweet music that caught and held him transfixed against the convolutions of the iron fence.
>
> The moon was above, lustrous and serene; vehicles and pedestrians were few; sparrows twittered sleepily in the eaves—for a little while the scene might have been a country churchyard. And the anthem that the organist played cemented Soapy to the iron fence, for he had known it well in the days when his life contained such things as mothers and roses and ambitions and friends and immaculate thoughts and collars.
>
> The conjunction of Soapy's receptive state of mind and the influence about the old church wrought a sudden and wonderful change in his soul. He viewed with swift horror the pit into which he had tumbled, the degraded days, unworthy desires, dead hopes, wrecked faculties and base motives that made up his existence. . . .

Soapy decided that he would pull himself out of the mire, but he felt a hand on his arm. He looked round and saw that his friend the cop had come at last. Next day the kind magistrate gave Soapy three months on the Island.

O. Henry was buried from The Little Church Around the Corner and his own funeral story had the sardonic twist that he gave to many of his tales. It is not known that he had expressed any preference in churches, but he had wandered in and out of Transfiguration and had detected the quality that made it remarkable in its city setting. His friends selected it as a suitable place for his funeral services. The author had only recently returned to town from Asheville, N. C., where he had gone for his health. He had missed New York and had longed for the rush of traffic, the quirk of circumstance and the city-bred types that people his stories. He had been back only a few days when he fell ill in his hotel apartment. Seizing the telephone, he was barely able to convey his plight to a friend, before collapsing on the bed. He was taken to the Polyclinic Hospital where he died on a Sunday morning, just as early communion mass was being said in The Little Church Around the Corner. He had asked the doctor to raise his pillow. "I don't want to go home in the dark," O. Henry had whispered as his life ebbed.

The funeral was set for 11 o'clock on a June morning in 1910. Dr. Houghton, an inveterate reader of the short story, was an admirer of O. Henry's work. He prepared to read the burial service without any foreknowledge that a mistake in the arrangements would bring a bride to the church to say her wedding vows at the hour set for the funeral. In the excitement of her wedding preparations Miss Ida Louise Crossley, of East Orange, N. J., had not even noticed that the author was dead. She had always said that she would be married in The Little Church Around the Corner. Once she had witnessed the wedding of a friend there, and had dropped in many times afterwards, impressed with its beauty and its peace. Her own rector was in Europe during the summer of 1910, so she arranged with her fiancé, Frederick C. Thomas, that the wedding should take place in the church of her fancy. It was not to be an elaborate affair but a small gathering of relatives and close friends. The wedding breakfast was to be given at the Holland House, a favourite hostelry of the period that served many of the brides of Transfiguration because of its handiness to the church.

The bridegroom's brother was the first to arrive on the scene. He was surprised to find a crowd gathered in the churchyard whose attire and demeanour suggested a funeral. Mr. Thomas sought Dr. Houghton in his office and reminded him that his brother's wedding had been set for 11 o'clock.

The rector realized at once what had happened. He explained that O. Henry's funeral was set for the same time by mistake and suggested that the wedding party be waylaid and sent on to the Holland House for an hour. The brother hurried out to the street, anxious lest the shadow of the hearse should fall across the bride's path. He was able to warn the guests as they arrived. In each case he explained the true state of affairs but urged them to keep all knowledge of the funeral from Miss Crossley. When the bridegroom arrived and jumped out of the car the truth was whispered in his ear. Momentary interest and comprehension flashed across his face. The name was one to evoke interest even then. Miss Crossley arrived at the same time and she was told that there had been some confusion in the arrangements. Another girl was to be married at 11 o'clock. She was reassured when she heard that Dr. Houghton would be ready to perform the ceremony for her at noon. She looked inquiringly at the sombre figures in the churchyard but her suspicions were not aroused. For an hour she chatted gaily with the wedding guests in the Holland House.

The pallbearers for O. Henry were Richard Harding Davis, John O'Hara Cosgrave, Walter Hines Page, Dr. John H. Finley, Will Irwin and Don C. Seitz. They had noticed the bridal party and had quickly realized the irony of it. Those who had known him best felt that this was the sort of *envoi* that would have piqued O. Henry's fancy. It was fantastically like a tale from his own pen. Had the cortège not been a little late in leaving the undertaking parlours on Fourth Avenue the two groups would inevitably have met. As it was, Miss Crossley in her summery silks was disappearing around the corner at Fifth Avenue when the hearse drove up to the lich-gate from the opposite direction. According to his custom at funerals, the rector of Transfiguration read *Crossing the Bar* over the bier of O. Henry. The author's body was being sent to North Carolina for burial and immediately after the brief service the cortège proceeded to the Pennsylvania Station. The funeral flowers had scarcely been removed when Miss Crossley and her party arrived, and the lighter fragrance of wedding bouquets took the place of the O. Henry wreaths. Once again The

Little Church Around the Corner was fulfilling its different functions with a tranquil recognition of life's complexities. There was nothing about the church to suggest that the wandering troubadour had made way for a Jersey bride. The guests, knowing the story, were all impressed by the event, but the bride was unconscious of the drama in which she had shared. Her chief concern was the thundershower that darkened the sky as she left the church. The sun had shone during O. Henry's funeral but lowering clouds cast grey shadows over the path of the bride.

Next day the newspapers carried routine accounts of the funeral and in an obscure corner was tucked a brief notice of Miss Crossley's wedding. There was nothing to relate the two in the public mind, nor did the majority of those who had attended the funeral service know what had happened. It was years before the story was pieced together and then only by a coincidence. George MacAdam, who had been at the funeral and observed the bridal party, mentioned the incident twelve years later in an article, "O. Henry's only Autobiographia," which appeared in *The New York Times Book Review*, and was later repeated in his history of the Little Church. By chance, the girl on whom the shadow of O. Henry's funeral had fallen, read the article. She was deeply interested and wrote to Mr. MacAdam. They met and she filled in all the missing links in the story. She told him that on the day after their wedding her husband had shown her a newspaper account of the funeral and had explained that this was the reason for the delay. Since it had not clouded the day, she accepted the news then with little concern, and both she and her husband felt that they had participated in a magic O. Henry tale, the last of a great series.

St. Joseph's Mortuary Chapel had only recently been consecrated and in its deep recesses the dead were hereafter to lie in the soft transfusion of light from the Transfiguration window, which had been moved from above the altar to become the central *motif* of the chapel. Much as his uncle had longed for the lich-gate, Dr. Houghton had looked forward to having a chapel where the stranger in the city who died in a cheerless hotel room might be

ᵐᵖ R L B   R L Boyer

ST. JOSEPH'S CHAPEL

given a decorous resting place until the time of the funeral services. He worked over the plan with the same care and passion for detail that he had expended on the Lady Chapel. In 1906 the vestry considered the proposal and a resolution was adopted favouring the addition of St. Joseph's to Transfiguration. It was built in the angle extension formed by the nave and the transept. Its octagonal tower may be seen at the east end of the church with a cross above it, one of the last touches of grace added to a building which had now rambled as far as space permitted across the old glebe land nurtured by the founder.

Appropriately enough, the chapel was designed as a memorial to him and was consecrated in November, 1908. During the intervening years all manner of people have been brought here for burial. The stage stars of fifty years ago have lain in state a step from the pews in which they worshipped when Booth and Jefferson strode into the church on Sunday mornings. Actors, writers, bishops, doctors, baseball players and artists—all have rested in the Gothic interior of this cosmopolitan chapel. Visitors from abroad who have died in the whirl of a heedless city have been buried here with the full benediction of the parish, and faded old down-and-outers have mopped their tears at the bier of a forgotten actress who once dazzled Broadway with her Camille. Some of the leading stars of this generation have stipulated that when they die they wish to lie in state in St. Joseph's Chapel, and one actress, who wants her vivacity to live in the minds of her admirers, has asked that no one shall see her face when the end comes.

The interior is twenty-two feet high, and hanging bronze lamps, shaped like the ancient crypt lamps with tongue-flamed light, are suspended, ever burning, from the ceiling. The walls are panelled with mahogany and the mouldings are traced in gold-leaf. Like the Lady Chapel, St. Joseph's is pure Gothic. The floor is of marble mosaic with the founder's initials pieced together before the altar. The Transfiguration window spreads a royal mantle of colour over the resting place of the dead, and its tinted beams stream into the nave through the grillwork of the gates given by Miss S. Adelina Moller in memory of her brother, Edwin Clarence Moller. Many mourners have knelt between the tall silver candlesticks given by the late Frank R. Ford, the junior warden, in memory of his first wife, Mrs. Sunshine Helen Ford, who died in November, 1923.

Bronze tablets on the walls commemorate some of those who have figured in the history of the church, and one of the first to be installed was dedicated to Walter William Griffin, who died in 1907. The inscription reads:

For thirty-five years postman for
Twenty-ninth Street

Father in Thy gracious keeping
leave we now Thy servant
sleeping.

All these years, while the church was becoming a widely known institution, the little postman with his sack bulging with mail had faithfully delivered the heavy batches of letters that came from different parts of the world to The Little Church Around the Corner. Like all of its old retainers, he had a special affection for the church. It pleased him to see stamps from foreign lands, for then he knew that the brides in far-off countries remembered the place where they had taken their wedding vows.

XIII

WAR DAYS AT TRANSFIGURATION

INDUSTRY and commerce were now beginning to jostle The Little Church Around the Corner. The brownstone fronts were at last giving way to tall lofts and skyscrapers. Fine old residences were being snuffed out in the wake of the wrecker. The Waldorf-Astoria looked like an antique among its ambitious neighbours, although considerable sentiment still clung to its baroque façades. The theatrical centre of town was well established at Times Square and the lights of the Gay White Way blazed in twinkling fantasies far up Broadway. The older generation of actors that gathered around the first Dr. Houghton had passed on, but their children and grandchildren were coming to the church for marriage and baptism. John Drew was still a popular figure on Broadway and the Barrymores were the reigning stars.

The residential quarters had shifted far uptown, although Gramercy Park and Washington Square still kept themselves green and intact, with old-fashioned dwellings and an occasional carriage and pair. Greenwich Village during this period was authentically bohemian and many struggling artists and writers, who have since attained fame, were living in its garrets. The old Tenderloin, which had been the first Dr. Houghton's particular care, was only an echo of its earlier self. Modernist architecture was casting its first shadows, with distant vistas of swinging towers and sharp corners, of honeycombed windows flashing the sunset's reflection, and silver needlepoints piercing the star-flecked sky at night. Architects were drawing fantastic plans of tunnels and aerial bridges, set-backs and tiered colossi that have strangely come to pass. The age of the combined church and skyscraper hotel was dawning, and the clergy sought for novelties to fill their pews on Sunday.

Golf, moving pictures and the motor car had all had their effect on church-going. A few of the old Episcopal churches lingered downtown, however, among the mounds and towers of Crœsus. Trinity, whose spire had once dominated Wall Street, was now sunk to a graceful bit of Gothic in the midst of aspiring modernism. St. Paul's ignored the flow of commerce around its old churchyard and prided itself on George Washington's pew. St. Marks-in-the-Bouwerie, the burial place of Peter Stuyvesant, remained a segment of early New York completely surrounded by slum. The poetic spire of Grace Church, that once stood at the head of Broadway, still had the sky for a background, although motor vans racketed past its cool, green garden. The Church of the Ascension held its ground close to some of the old homes of Washington Square, and the surmounting tip of Transfiguration's cross was now in provocative silhouette. The clustering towers took on a new harmony, huddled against an arid wall of steel and concrete, a tiny cathedral, dim and celestial, fashioned in the heart of a sprawling factory. North and south, east and west, the four-storey houses were no more, and a jagged skyline had taken their place. The gardens and stoops were replaced by pavements, and occa-sional window boxes or pots of ivy were the only remaining touches of ver-dancy. The flowers no longer grew so well with the shadows of tall buildings falling on the *close* of The Little Church Around the Corner. Michael found that the shade, the dust and the gasolene were combining to kill the blooms that had once stood like proud maids of honour for every June bridal party. The gardening technique was changed and more bushes and shrubs were planted, so that the churchyard might remain green and shady, though its colours were less gay. The birds still haunted their rustic houses in the elms. When the migrations were on, they came in flocks, chirping and splashing in the fountain, then soaring off to unknown destinations.

After the United States entered the war, the church was swept into a fresh period of activity. Nurses were confirmed, bandages were rolled, sol-diers were married by the score. Dr. Houghton sponsored the Allied Officers' Club on East Thirtieth Street, where rooms and meals were furnished for military men at reasonable rates. Miss Harriet Parks Stevens, now the choir mother at Transfiguration, was in charge. The winter of 1917-18 was one of the coldest and most severe ever experienced in New York. The temperature sank to thirteen below zero and the snowfall gave it ranking among the years of blizzards. Railroads were tied up, river transportation was blocked by ice floes, and the elevated trains and subways were all hampered for want of power. Coal was scarce and the charity guilds of Transfiguration worked at high pressure alleviating distress among the poor. Dr. Houghton and his curates went all over town on errands of mercy. Industry closed down for ten days and the city shivered in icy inactivity. The Hoover food campaign was in progress and Broadway was a dark and lifeless thoroughfare for the time being. Fifth Avenue was dimmer than in its old gas-lit days.

The work of the parish had doubled and the run of war marriages was on, with Dr. Houghton exercising a restraining hand on the countless couples who marched hopefully into his study seeking his priestly offices. These were not the most cheerful days in the history of the church, for many of the brides wept on the ribboned marriage certificate scroll handed them by Miss Hanlon, as they thought of their husbands leaving for overseas. Bleak tragedy had cast its shadow on some of those who sought advice and guidance. There were war complications, jealousies, estrangements and disrupted emotions. Strange stories were told in the little office, and both Dr. Houghton and Miss Hanlon lent aid and comfort to scores who were fumbling in the dark.

Because of the secrecy of the confessional no one will ever know how many reconciliations have been effected by the rectors of The Little Church Around the Corner, but its reputation as the home of romance and marriage has brought it all manner of emotional problems to solve. Its advisory offices, however, have by no means been confined solely to affairs of the heart and a variety of difficulties have been straightened out in the busy quarters adjoining the church. In the days before the Actors' Guild had been formed, the people of the stage brought diversified problems to The Little Church Around the Corner. Actresses, out of work and desperate, found solace and aid in the confessional, and at times employment was put their way. Stage couples who were divorced and who could not be married there received such consolation and advice as Dr. Houghton could give them. He helped them to patch up their difficulties, and to make compromises for the sake of their children. As an avowed opponent of divorce he believed that the married should stick together, however great the provocation to separate.

The armistice brought soldiers trooping home and there was another marked advance in the wedding statistics. But Dr. Houghton's health was now failing. Functionaries long associated with the church were passing on, one by one. James Potter Dod, the organist, died in 1917, just before the Christmas services in which he had always taken pride. He had been a devoted adherent since the surpliced choir was installed in 1881. The music at Transfiguration had always been excellent and Mr. Dod had had much to do with maintaining its standard. After his death a memorial tablet was placed for him, not in the mortuary chapel where the others are, but close to the organ pipes, symbol of his devotion. It bears the inscription: *A faithful communicant, a devoted choir master, a zealous worker for righteousness.* The next of the old faces to disappear was that of William Franklin Adams, sacristan of the church for forty years, who died a few months after Mr. Dod. The six altar candles are a memorial to this gentle, scholarly soul who had attended with infinite care to the details of the ceremonial. The parish house was his home and the church his entire world. He took pride in the possessions of Transfiguration and jealously guarded the handsome communion vessels and the vestments, particularly the ceremonial set given to Dr. Houghton in 1913. They were made by the Anglican Sisters of St. Mary's Convent, Peekskill, and the damask for the chasuble was woven in silver and gold thread on looms at Lyons. Crosses of gold and jewelled opal centres adorn these vestments, which are still used by Dr. Ray on ceremonial occasions. William Judson Minor, sexton and undertaker for thirty years, died shortly before Mr. Dod and Mr. Adams, and another tablet was put up in St. Joseph's Chapel for him. He had succeeded James Rappleyea, the first sexton, and Victor Sharkey in turn succeeded Mr. Minor. Miss Jennie T. Draper completed the little group of retainers who had worked with the first Dr. Houghton, and whose lives were completely bound up with the church. She was the guiding spirit of the Sunday School for fifty-one years and when she disappeared from her pew within a few months of Dr. Houghton's death, it seemed as if the church had lost one of its rare possessions. Miss Draper always played the organ on Ascension Day; and one of the members of the Lenten choir was Mrs. William Robert Mowe, who still comes regularly to the church with her niece, Miss Alice Welles.

Mrs. Strombom was an increasingly active figure in the church and rectory as her father's health declined. She brought dash and liveliness to his darker days and was a spirited buffer between him and all outside annoyances. She was a tall and handsome woman, a vivid brunette with dark eyes, an olive complexion and black hair. Mrs. Strombom was humorous and quick in repartee and she met church problems with considerable vigour. She was notoriously generous and, during her twenty-five years at the rectory, conducted an open-handed ménage. Her father teased her about her shopping expeditions, for Mrs. Strombom could never resist the things she saw in the shops, and she filled the rectory with impulsive purchases. She frequently treated her guests to surprises in the way of novel table effects. Even before coloured glass and linen had become popular, she varied conventional damask and crystal with a table done all in lavender, green or rose, as the spirit moved her. She surrounded herself with bright colours and was at all times a positive personality in the affairs of the parish.

Mrs. Strombom nursed her father devotedly and gave up much of her own life to his interests. Dr. Houghton, now grown grey and portly, celebrated the fiftieth anniversary of his ordination as a priest on May 19, 1921. He was so weak that he had to be aided out to a chair near the fountain. A procession of clergy from far and near filed in through the lich-gate to do him honour, winding in double lines towards the church. Here were old associates, fellow churchmen, friends and colleagues, assembled for his Golden

Jubilee. He trembled as he rose to meet the oncoming line, and with halting step he led the processional inside, where already the pews were packed with parishioners, actors, brides of the church, and other friends of long standing. The high altar was banked with flowers. The Lady Chapel and St. Joseph's Chapel stood as monuments to the care he had lavished on the heritage left him by his uncle. Only a few days before, looking around the familiar interior of the church, he had said:

> I cannot recall any step taken that was not in accord
> with the founder's plans—nothing that would not receive
> his full approbation. That has been my aim and I have
> tried to fulfill it faithfully.

His thoughts drifted into the past as he saw the foremost stage stars of the day standing in pews under the memorial windows to Booth, Mansfield and Montague. With twitching lips he read the gospel, standing between two acolytes with lighted tapers. The Rt. Rev. Thomas F. Gailor preached the sermon. Holy Communion was celebrated by the Rev. Shirley Carter Hughson, Superior of the Order of the Holy Cross, and the Rt. Rev. William T. Manning, Bishop of the Diocese of New York, made a congratulatory address and pronounced the benediction.

Miss Elsie Ferguson stepped forward and gave him a hand-illumined vellum scroll inscribed with the felicitations of the Actors' Equity Association. Grant Stewart and Charles A. Stevenson, on behalf of The Lambs, gave him a silver loving cup. Dr. Houghton had kept intact the theatrical following that had made the church remarkable. In an interview on the day of his jubilee he voiced his personal views on this subject:

> I don't see how a man can criticize people he doesn't
> know, in any Christlike spirit. I have known so many
> actors and actresses as fine ladies and gentlemen that I
> can't believe that any man who condemns them all really
> knows them. Even the little girls who dance in musical

shows are not to be condemned by any man because they wear short costumes. I have had young stage girls come to me for advice and I know them to be respectable. I can't criticize musical comedies of to-day because I have not been to a theatre for many years. But as to the actors themselves, I know of no better class of people.

After his jubilee Dr. Houghton failed noticeably. He went south for his health but there was no improvement. It was only now and again that he was well enough to take part in the services. Letters poured in from all quarters of the world, many of them from couples he had married years before and who had read of his jubilee. He was virtually an invalid by Easter Sunday, 1923, and on that day he said prophetically to his daughter: "I know I shall never go into the church again until I am carried there." When the service was ended in the church, the choir came in to the rectory and sang for him.

During Dr. Ray's seminary days he had come in contact with Dr. Houghton and, when the time came for the selection of a vicar, he was the man on whom his elder colleague sought to cast the mantle of Transfiguration. At the rector's request Dr. Ray was invited by the vestry to be vicar, and on April 15, 1923, Dr. Houghton wrote to his parishioners presenting his new assistant. He recalled how he had been summoned to the church himself shortly before his uncle's death. He said that the time had come when he felt unable to fulfill all the duties of the parish. And so:

> I am presenting to you the Rev. Jackson H. Randolph Ray, who by my wish your vestry have so graciously allotted me, who will, I believe, be strong in the work necessary to be carried out in this part of God's vineyard. I commend him to you . . . I commend him to you with my love . . . the vestry has been kind enough to say that I shall rest, or work as it pleases me, and I am grateful for this permission to do so. . . . And to you, my dear friend,

whom I am placing before the people as my chief helpmate in this work, I bid Godspeed, and may God the Father, and may God the Son, and may God the Holy Ghost, give you day by day and hour by hour, the blessing you need, and the blessing that will be required for that work of great importance which shall rest upon your shoulders . . . God bless you . . .

A few days later Dr. Houghton realized that the end was near. He told his nurse that he was dying, and Mrs. Strombom rushed to get Dr. Ray to administer the last sacrament. It was taken from the tabernacle on the altar of the Lady Chapel, before which his prayers had risen for many years. He died in Dr. Ray's arms. His funeral was held on April 21 and four requiem masses were said in Transfiguration. Sunlight filtered through the windows, a violet and blue mist, tinged with amber fire that lit the banks of lilies to a tawny radiance. A blanket of lilies and orchids lay across the coffin at the chancel rail. Pews were reserved close to the Booth window for members of The Lambs and The Players. The Rt. Rev. Herbert S. Shipman conducted the burial service, assisted by Dr. Ray and the Rev. Dr. Henry Lubeck. John Drew, who had been married in Transfiguration, walked down the aisle as an honorary pallbearer, along with George Arliss, Otis Skinner, Grant Stewart, A. O. Brown, Frank Gillmore, John E. Hazzard, Commodore Elbridge T. Gerry, Haley Fiske, Dr. Samuel W. Lambert, Newcomb Carlton, Dr. Edward Cussler, Robert W. Mowe and Judge Robert L. Luce. Out of tribute to Dr. Houghton, the Police Department closed Twenty-ninth Street to traffic while the services were being held. The second rector of the Church of the Transfiguration was buried in Kensico Cemetery beside the wife whose memory he had kept green for twenty-one years.

XIV

THE THIRD RECTOR IS INSTALLED

A BITTER controversy on dogma was now raging through the diocese of New York. The Rev. Dr. Percy Stickney Grant, one of the picturesque figures of the Episcopal Church at this time, was questioning the Virgin Birth from the pulpit of the Church of the Ascension, a courtly priest tilting against tradition. The stir caused by Dr. Grant's historic sermon in defiance of Bishop Manning had scarcely died down before the Rev. Dr. William Norman Guthrie incurred diocesan ostracism over the pagan dances and the eurythmics of the vesper services at St. Marks-on-the-Bouwerie. The old antagonisms of the High and Low Church elements, which had been banked for many years, glowed again for a time and then burned down in the diocese.

Into this atmosphere stepped the new clergyman from the south, magnetic and imaginative, his wordly sense harmoniously aligned with his essential orthodoxy. Dr. Ray had been carefully chosen by Dr. Houghton as the third rector to carry on the traditions of the Church of the Transfiguration. His first public announcement presaged the course he was to follow:

> The policy of broad charity and love which the founder, and later, Dr. Houghton, built in with every stone of the Church of the Transfiguration will be continued. I am aware that people not only in New York, but in all parts of the country as well, have a very tender regard for this church, and I should like to see that feeling kept up. I want people to use the church without regard to any narrow ideas. That is to be the course of the church—to keep up its beautiful services and loyalty to the faith.

Dr. Ray was no stranger to New York. He knew the city intimately and in many aspects. Years earlier he had haunted The Little Church Around the Corner and had formed an attachment for it that later seemed to him to be almost prophetic. He plunged into the work of the parish with an energy attuned to the city that now thundered at his gate. Maintaining the ceremonial at its highest level, he pursued the simple gospel of charity and the open door that had always been characteristic of the church. Dr. Ray came to a New York that had changed greatly since that Sunday morning three-quarters of a century earlier when a small group of people had strolled up Love Lane, prayer books in hand, and had surrounded another young clergyman filled with enthusiasm for his task. Motor cars now rolled up to the church instead of carriages. Prohibition had set its mark on the social life of the generation. Radio was sweeping the country and 2,500,000 receiving sets were already in use, with many sermons and church services being broadcast. The drive to complete the Cathedral of St. John the Divine was on, and the Rev. Dr. John Roach Straton was denouncing sin in the manner of Dr. Talmage back in the '80's.

Michael's hair was now grey, but his churchyard bloomed with everlasting freshness as the hose whirled a cooling spray on the grass, and elephant ears rose like green umbrellas around the fountain where the birds still splashed, though fewer in number. Men's attire, which had evolved less speedily than women's since the crinoline age, was now being fashioned for more casual wear than the swallow-tails, silk vests and flinty-bosomed shirts of thirty years before. Men dared to come to church in Panamas or felt hats. They arrayed themselves in heather mixtures, in greys, browns, blues and light weaves, at the same time admitting the soft collar to an honoured place in the wardrobe of the well-dressed man about town. New York itself, its architecture, its shops and customs, had changed to an incredible degree. The tempo of the city was now swift and clanging, where once it had been slow and subdued. Its turrets soared skyward, a vast grey fresco tipped with silver and gold, shaded with black and beryl.

THE REVEREND DOCTOR RANDOLPH RAY
THIRD RECTOR

THE THIRD RECTOR IS INSTALLED

The incoming rector of Transfiguration was essentially a modern, aware of the new social currents and in sympathy with the sentiment and tradition of the church. There were many factors in his upbringing and experience that had contributed to his equipment for the incumbency. He had not come to the church by way of the rigid path of straight clericism but by an accumulation of experiences that have lent colour and sophistication to his ministry. As far back as he can remember, Dr. Ray had an urge to come north. Vital and ambitious, slumberous days under the cotton sun did not suit him temperamentally and he hankered after the swift pace of the metropolis. He was born on June 11, 1886, in Madison County, Mississippi, the son of Captain Jackson Harvelle Ray, a cotton planter and Confederate soldier. He is a direct descendant of William Randolph, who was Councillor of Turkey Island, Virginia, at the close of the seventeenth century, and of a distinguished line of Virginian and English ancestors. Dr. Ray was the seventh son of a seventh son and his father read destiny into that. "You must attain," he would tell his small son, until the idea was firmly planted in his youthful mind. The rector's earliest recollection is of being in plantation cotton fields surrounded by just such Negroes as appeared in *The Green Pastures*. His own black mammy was a perfect type.

Dr. Ray was educated in private schools in the south and was graduated from Emory and Henry College in Virginia on St. Barnabas' Day, 1905, always a portentous date for him. It was while he was in college that he gave up the idea of studying for the church, a career that his mother had mapped out for him. He had shown a slight ecclesiastical bent as a boy, but had lost this feeling in college. At last his desire to come north prevailed, and he first saw The Little Church Around the Corner when he was eighteen years old. He felt at home in it at once. The sense of harmony that has touched many visitors made a profound impression on the youth from the south. He had come to New York to study medicine, but before long he realized that surgery and pathology were definitely repugnant to him. His father had advised him to take up law, so now he turned his attention to Blackstone. He soon discovered that the law held no fascination for him as a career. The poets were more to his taste. However, his days at Columbia College were agreeable, and he belonged to a group that worshipped at the feet of Brander Matthews. He had become profoundly interested in the drama and went to the theatre as often as his studies permitted. He acted with considerable success in amateur theatricals and was given a vigorous voice training by Ben Greet.

All of this he had thoroughly enjoyed, but when it became apparent to him that the law was not his métier he turned to letters. Dr. Matthews gave him a note of introduction to the editor of one of Munsey's magazines and this started Dr. Ray on the journalistic road. He did a variety of magazine articles and then joined the staff of *The Brooklyn Eagle*. He was doing newspaper work during the financial crash of 1907. Up to that time he had been going through a period of disillusionment and scepticism, and was virtually an atheist. Strangely enough, he dropped his cynicism during his newspaper days. He came into contact with men who had lost everything in the crash and he was impressed by their spiritual faith. His thoughts went back to his earlier days when the church had seemed his predestined career. He decided that he would rather be a clergyman than anything else, and, at the same time, he thought that he would rather minister at The Little Church Around the Corner than in any other parish. Looking back on these years, Dr. Ray believes that every step in his life must have been planned by a higher power, for his assorted experiences have contributed directly to his capacity as a priest. He entered the General Theological Seminary and soon realized that at last he had found the career for which he was best equipped. He missed the theatre but enjoyed his studies and the atmosphere of the Seminary. He was graduated in 1911. In the following year the Right Rev. David H. Greer ordained him a priest in the Cathedral of St. John the Divine. His first charge was a curacy under Dr. Lubeck at the Church of Zion and St. Timothy. He was thoroughly familiar with the Episcopal churches throughout the city by this time, and Transfiguration had become something of an obsession with him. He would tell his fellow clerics: "There is only one church of which I should like to be rector and that is The Little Church Around the Corner." So that the experience he had when he dropped in to the church one day is perhaps less miraculous than it seems. Dr. Ray has a strong psychic sense and believes in signs and portents. Many incidents within his own experience have tended to strengthen his metaphysical leanings. And not the least of these was his vision as he settled himself in a pew, drinking deep of the beauties of the church, his eyes roving from the memorial windows to the angels on the altar and the Venetian mosaics above the chancel rail. He now recalls that it was as if he had fallen asleep. He was watching himself at the altar and then in the pulpit, exactly as he was to function ten years later. He went back and told Dr. Lubeck of his experience. He informed the rector that he had had a perfect sense of unity when he walked under the lich-gate and inside the door of the church. "I am sure that I am bound to be there," he said, and Dr. Lubeck listened sympathetically and agreed with him. Years later, when he was being installed, Dr. Lubeck recalled his words and his sense of certainty on that occasion.

Life has always been slightly touched with the miraculous for Dr. Ray and no one could make him believe that there was not an element of predestination in his accession to the incumbency. In 1914 he went back to the south to act as rector of St. Andrew's Church in Bryan, Texas. Before leaving he met Miss Evangeline Adams for the first time and she read his horoscope and told him that he was not making a mistake in accepting the offer. Her predictions about the death of his father and various other events in his life made such a profound impression on him that he has consulted her frequently since then. His ministry at Bryan was a new and interesting experience for the young rector. Although more or less cut off from the cosmopolitan interests on which he thrived, he made many friends and kept alive his interest in the stage through the occasional visits of stock companies to a nearby town. He would drive over and bring the actors back to dinner at his home. The students of the agricultural college which he served as chaplain began to talk of his preaching, and they liked the understanding young man who had come among them. In due time he was transferred to the Cathedral of St. Matthew in Dallas, where he served as dean. Here he had an excellent chance to exercise his talents and he achieved distinction as a preacher and personality. St. Matthew's became one of the largest and most active parishes in the Southwest, trebling the number of its communicants. There was a war aviation camp at Dallas, and touring theatrical companies which played there kept him in touch with Broadway. He organized social affairs for the actors at the rectory and occasionally amateur shows were staged in the parish house.

While still at the Cathedral in Dallas, Dr. Ray came north and was married to Miss Mary Elmendorf Watson at St. Thomas's on July 20, 1922. She was the grand-daughter of Dr. Eugene A. Hoffman, a distinguished scholar and philanthropist who was dean of the General Theological Seminary from 1876 to 1901. Her father was also a clergyman, so that when she returned from Dallas with Dr. Ray in 1923 to preside at the rectory of Transfiguration, she was completely at home in the Episcopal tradition. Mrs. Strombom was one of her friends, and she had had a link with the church long before she met and married Dr. Ray. Things moved smoothly in the parish from the start, the Rays fitting gracefully into their new environment and the advent of Kathryna later on bringing a gay note to the rectory that it had not had before, since she was the first child to be brought up in it. Kathryna was born in Pittsfield on August 21, 1924, and was baptized with the name of one of the first Dutch babies to come to Nieuw Amsterdam. As a descendant of the Martinus Hoffman who came to the United States from Holland in 1640, her parents chose Hoffman for her middle name.

Like her husband, Mrs. Ray enjoys the theatre and is frequently hostess to Broadway celebrities, as well as to the prelates and guests of social prominence and diversified interests who gather at her dinner table. Tall, dark and extremely good looking, with clear brown eyes and a serene manner, she goes her way, gracious and tolerant in all her contacts. She likes golf, swimming, riding and most forms of outdoor exercise. Dr. Ray is less athletic in his tastes, preferring to garden at *Elm Ridge*, his 130-acre place at Litchfield, Conn., or to walk when he is in town. Although a dignified and remote figure while performing the offices of the church, he is an affable and open-minded priest and friend, equally at ease in lounging country clothes or the cassock of his office. He does not hedge himself with ceremony, but with bland manner and humorous eyes meets a bewildering variety of problems day after day. His easy approach paves the way for the suppliant and the sinner. He is friends with all manner of people, and is as much in his element chatting in a theatre lobby with Otto H. Kahn, or any other persistent first-nighter, as he is holding confessional in his small, book-lined study. For Dr. Ray is a man of catholic tastes and it has been said of him that his mind resembles the interior of The Little Church Around the Corner, a storehouse of assorted belongings. He goes to the theatre frequently and has a healthy interest in the drama. The church is a passion with him. Like his predecessors, his eyes feast on it with constant delight and he is never tired of planning new ways to dignify and adorn the interior. Not long ago a stranger dropped in late at night who was shown every nook and cranny, and had the church described to him in Dr. Ray's most poetical manner. He was an editor from British Columbia and it was not until he had returned to his home and had written an article on the church for his paper that he learned the identity of his enthusiastic guide.

Dr. Ray maintains the old rule of the church of being accessible, and his days are filled with ceaseless activity. Aided by his secretary, Miss Grace A. Mills, he attends to his vast correspondence, writing in engaging vein to the amazing number of former brides who send *vignettes* of their lives to The Little Church Around the Corner. Weddings, baptisms and funerals follow one another in close succession and it is a problem many days to fit in all the marriage appointments. Dr. Ray devotes considerable time in the afternoons to his parish calls. He prepares his sermons with great care. Because of his own writing experience he has a facility for words, but his sermons are studiously thought out and are delivered in fluent and graceful English.

Kathryna and her blue cocker spaniel *Raggles* lend considerable charm to the busy church and rectory. She is a vivacious child, with brown curls, who likes to dress up as a bride now and again from force of example. She has unveiled a memorial window, is friends with many stage stars and possesses a doll's house second only to Queen Mary's. It was a Christmas present given to her in 1929 by Mrs. Drury, who was a cousin of Mrs. Ray. The house is a miniature reproduction of one in Berkeley Square and, happily enough, one of Kathryna's greatest friends is Leslie, the little daughter of Leslie Howard, who played the part of the dreamy Colonial in *Berkeley Square*. Mrs. Drury's husband belonged to the family that gave its name to the London lane which has figured in the history of the drama since 1663.

The doll's house is eight feet long and five feet high, and was designed by the cabinetmaker who made Queen Mary's model. Mrs. Drury took two years to equip the fourteen rooms with treasures from different European countries. It contains 2,000 pieces, including Chippendale and Tudor furniture, Royal Worcester china, rare pictures and *objets d'art*. The house has a garage and a fashionable motor car, a lawn with trees and garden furniture, a roof garden, electric lights, running water, linen in the closets, liquor in the cellar, a library, and all the domestic appliances of the modern housekeeper. It has a master, a mistress, three children and a grandmother, as well as a chauffeur and a staff of servants, all attired with the full elegance of their station. Kathryna's own grandmother, Mrs. Jackson H. Ray, a gentlewoman of the Old South and a descendant of Sir Alexander Spottswood, Colonial Governor of Virginia, lives at the rectory with the son who eventually followed the career she had selected for him as a child.

XV

MEMORIES

Dr. RAY had been at The Little Church Around the Corner for less than six months when the seventy-fifth anniversary of the founding was celebrated with special services. Externally the church had preserved the rustic charm of its early days but, inside, it was now a storehouse of treasures, mellowed with age and tradition. It threw its softening shade on hurrying throngs who gave less heed to churchgoing than did the contemporaries of Serena Keeler. Mrs. Randall C. Hall thought of her mother and her father as she walked under the lich-gate to attend the anniversary services. She was now old herself, but from the daguerreotypes in her home, and her mother's reminiscences, she could imagine that slight figure with swaying crinoline promising to love, honour and obey George Eyland, in a setting that was much plainer than that on which her eye now rested. She and her daughter, Miss Margaret Pynchon Hall, were guests of honour, and Miss Anna Houghton, another link with the old days of the church, sat in the rector's pew.

A year later there was another celebration for the closing of the jubilee year and people came from long distances to attend the services. More than two thousand weddings had been solemnized during the year and almost as many baptisms. On this occasion a bronze tablet was unveiled in memory of Miss Jennie T. Draper, the gift of an alumni association made up of the boys she had taught in the Sunday School. She had been part and parcel of the church for more than half a century. Many physical changes in Transfiguration and its surroundings were noted at the jubilee. Another period of expansion had just ended. The rectory, which had long had a stoop like the rest of the neighbourhood, was remodelled and modernized. The church was painted and stuccoed, and new heating and electric plants were installed. The parish house, with activities that had again outgrown the accommodation, was given some repairs, which leave it still inadequate and outmoded for the needs of the church. Frank R. Ford, the junior warden, arranged for the restoration of the *close* and its maintenance by a landscape artist. It was re-graded, its outlines were completely altered to conform with the changes in the rectory, and new shrubs were planted to maintain its verdancy in the heart of a dusty city.

There was no more familiar figure at the church during these years than Miss Susan Ruth Budd, who wandered in and out with *Bunda*, an Italian Lupina that had belonged to John Barrymore. She was one of those who had attached herself to Transfiguration from sheer affection and delight in its charm. Miss Budd was so proprietary that when the spirit moved her she would show visitors over the church, drawing attention to the aspects she preferred herself. She had been the Aldrich family governess and was quite a character in her way, sticking to the garments and traditions of an earlier generation. But she had a taste for feminism, too, and drove her friends to the polls. She was the first person to live at the Martha Washington Hotel and, being so close at hand, she took to dropping in at Transfiguration. She would dip with interest into the affairs of the church, a small and patrician figure with high buttoned boots and a commanding air. Among the rhododendrons in the *close* is a marble statue of the Madonna and Child with the inscription:

Susan Ruth Budd 1847–1926
She loved God, His Church, His Birds and His Flowers.

This is the memorial put up by her friends, one that she would have approved, for she loved the garden and watched the changing seasons with constant enthusiasm for its scenic effects. *Bunda* was carried away under a blanket of flowers and cremated after her death. This was her own wish, for the dog and the church had been her two interests. She was a communicant of the parish for forty years.

imp RLB   R L Boyer

OUR LADY OF THE GARDEN

MEMORIES

In spite of the residential sweep uptown, many of the old family names remained on the pews of Transfiguration, and among those still ushered in are Miss Julia and Miss Mary Kent, whose father was treasurer for many years; Miss Helen Sands, who can remember when the first Dr. Houghton asked the congregation to kneel at the Incarnatus in the Creed, and Mrs. Mowe, who used to sing in the Lenten choir. The Drapers, McAllisters, Mollers, Pells, Campbell Clarks, Livingstons, Arnolds, Schleys, Candlers, Lows, Schroeders, Roosevelts, Nicolls, Reeses, Howlands, Clinton Browns, Hayes, and the Chamberlaines are all represented on the parish rolls. Miss Ruth Draper, the *diseuse*, was baptized in Transfiguration and her family has been associated with the church almost from the days of its foundation.

With its nucleus of old parishioners, it has at the same time become an international church, linked with many lands and peoples. Letters, sentimental and reminiscent, drift in from the far corners of the earth to this little haven of peace. The cycle of life interlocks at its threshold and its children's children come back to see the shrine that has taken such hold of one generation after another. It is not unusual for a bride to have a quiet figure steal out of a pew and wish her well, recalling that she was married in Transfiguration many years ago and is back on a romantic pilgrimage. One old couple sat hand in hand in the chantry, watching a honey-haired girl in white satin taking her wedding vows. As she walked down the aisle, the older woman rushed forward and embraced her. She and her husband had come from California to celebrate their golden wedding and, finding another couple being married at the same hour fifty years later, the wife could not restrain her emotion.

Encounters of this sort are so common in The Little Church Around the Corner that they are scarcely noticed. Hundreds of silver-haired couples return on anniversaries and vacation trips, and some are so old that they look in vain for the spot where they were married. With faded eyes they contemplate an interior that has changed beyond belief. They find the Lady Chapel a quiet and soothing place for prayer, and the brides' chapel a golden shrine for reverie. One couple, married in the church thirty years ago, who live in the Far West, have come across the continent three times to see their children married in The Little Church Around the Corner. And a grandmother, married fifty years ago, was recently her grand-daughter's matron of honour at the altar where she had taken her own wedding vows. Footprints of babies and other sentimental tokens of affection are sent to the church from time to time, and an architect reproduced Transfiguration on a Christmas card with which he announced that he and his wife were still happy after a long lapse of years. When they cannot come back they send letters that give a clear picture of the impression the church has made on them. One woman whose husband was dying wrote asking that prayers be said for him "at the blessed altar that has brought such happiness to us both." A naval officer in Honolulu declared that it was just like a new honeymoon each time he and his wife came to New York and saw The Little Church Around the Corner again. A Western couple sent word that they had made five trips from Portland, Ore., to celebrate their anniversary at the church, and hoped to continue the custom as long as they were able to travel. They "would not miss it for worlds."

The brides of long ago are sometimes bewildered by all the new possessions the church has acquired, although the changes have been gradual and harmonious. The altar itself, with its reredos of Caen stone, is the object of primary interest and importance as visitors walk into the church. It was enlarged and improved in 1903 by Mrs. Sarah J. Zabriskie in memory of her mother, who died in 1894. The central division of the reredos represents the Transfiguration; at either side are figures of St. Matthew and St. Luke. Above is the crucifix, between figures of the Blessed Virgin and St. John. The tabernacle, given by Mrs. John L. Adams and Mrs. Charles Swan, gleams with jewels. The carpet leading to the altar is cardinal red and the whole effect of the chancel is one of warmth and brilliance. Flanking the altar are the subdued windows placed there by the Altar Society in memory of its first president, Miss Ann Aurora Ballow, who held the office for twenty years. Each has the figure of an angel swinging a censer, and underneath is the inscription: "Holy, Holy, Holy, Lord God of Sabaoth." The mosaics over the lectern and pulpit represent the Blessed Virgin and the Archangel Gabriel. They were made in Venice from old paintings and were the gift of William C. Prime. On one of the pillars dividing the nave from the transept hangs a valuable miniature of the Crucifixion, brought from Rome by Mme. de Verdi. The silver sanctuary bell was the gift of Miss Mary Chamberlaine in memory of her sister, Mrs. Benjamin Fabens. The crucifix which hangs close to the pulpit was presented by Miss Georgiana Howland and Miss A. R. Howland, daughters of the Rev. Dr. Robert S. Howland, who founded the Church of the Heavenly Rest.

The deep and glowing crimson of the figure in the St. Faith window has no counterpart in this country outside of the Metropolitan Museum, for it is a rare piece of fourteenth century stained glass with historic association. The window was taken from a Belgian church destroyed during the Napoleonic Wars. It is a memorial to David Loney Bruce-Brown from his mother and brother. Installed near the pulpit, the window faces the transept which, in itself, suggests a quiet oratory in one of the ancient Venetian churches whose steps lead down to the water's edge. Its rare and faded pictures in heavy gold frames are matched by the Stations of the Cross, fifteenth century paintings that once hung in a chapel in Rome. The windows of the Beatitudes were installed in the chantry in 1902, a memorial by the second Dr. Houghton to the founder. In the next year he installed the Rood Wall beneath the chancel arch as a memorial to his wife, and supplemented this with a window copied from a Murillo Madonna.

The narthex and chapel screens are Gothic, with elaborate tracery. In two large niches are carved and gilded statues of St. Joachim and St. Anne, with smaller statues along the upper arcade of the screen, representing St. George, John the Baptist, Elizabeth, Peter and Paul. The old organ gallery was retained in modified form to contain the echo section of the new organ, which was used for the first time on Christmas Eve, 1927. It is enclosed in a case harmonizing with the screens given by Mrs. Eleanor DeForest Boteler in memory of her brother, Elijah P. Smith, who was senior warden of the church for many years. They were suggested by the rood screens in Lord Shaftsbury's Chapel at Wimborne and in St. Edward's Church, Leeds. Mr. Smith was a cotton broker who died in 1926, at the age of eighty-seven. He was a faithful adherent of the church for fifty years. The wrought iron gates at either side of the choir are memorials installed by Miss Evelyn Breslin for her parents, Mr. and Mrs. James H. Breslin, and her sister, Mrs. Grant Shepherd, all of whom were communicants of the parish for years.

The pulpit of Transfiguration, which supplanted the old one of carved wood in 1890, is a memorial to the Rev. Dr. William Staunton and Mrs. Staunton, given by their daughter, Mrs. Thomas Bloodgood Peck. The lectern is a memorial to Lucy Robbins Draper, and the Litany Desk was given by Mr. and Mrs. Peck in memory of Mary Frances Peck. The elaborate window to the second Dr. Houghton, which shows him celebrating mass, was given by his daughter, Mrs. Strombom. There are two baptismal fonts in Transfiguration, the newer one being in the Gothic baptistery, with its seven little stained glass windows representing the heavenly hosts; the older one, in the Chapel of the Holy Family, close to the brides' altar. A great many babies whose names came to be well known in later years have been baptized at the old font. One of the earliest memorials in the church is to a child. Clarence Pell was born in 1871 and died when he was three. His parents gave a memorial window with a child's head and angel wings, which may now be seen in the vestibule of the transept. Across from it is another old memorial to José Maria Munoz, a Spanish actor whose history is obscure. A peculiar tradition has grown up about this window. Its central theme is a wreath of evergreens studded with bits of quartz. The story has spread that the wreath is sprinkled with uncut diamonds and there are signs that an attempt has been made to cut the glass in order to get at the mythical gems. It is known as the Diamond Window.

The services at Transfiguration are conducted with a strict regard to ceremonial. Dr. Ray has infused a certain degree of drama into the ritual at

Christmas and Easter. The crucifix from Oberammergau is used only once a year—on Good Friday. The church is draped in black and, at the end of the three hour passion service, the lights are dimmed until only the crucifix shines in the surrounding gloom. The choir sings the old reproaches and the bell is tolled thirty-three times, signifying Christ's age at the time of His death. As the tolling ends the lights come slowly on until they reach full strength. There is no celebration of Communion on Good Friday.

On Easter Eve the church is pitch dark again at vespers. The symbolism of striking fire from the flint is carried out and the processional starts with three candles in the darkness, the choir intoning *Jesus Christ, the Light of the World* as the Paschal candle is lighted. The acolyte touches his taper to all the candles on the altar, one after another, until their flickering flames dart like fiery streamers through the darkness. Now soft light suffuses the chancel and shadowy forms in vestments move about the altar. The church is suddenly flooded with light and all the saints and figures in stained glass emerge from the gloom in glowing colours.

On Palm Sunday a crucifer knocks loudly at the door and the choir files into the palm-filled church, the choristers singing the antiphonal Hosannas. On Maundy Thursday vigil is kept at the brides' altar. Women wearing the veil kneel before it, keeping watch in Gethsemane. On Easter Sunday there are festal processions and special music. The choir, always known for the excellence of its boy choristers, is under the direction of Frederick Rocke, who is both organist and choirmaster. The music of the church is in keeping with its dignified ceremonial, and the midnight mass on Christmas Eve brings throngs through the lich-gate to a softly-illumined church. Outside, passersby linger before its snowy eaves and gleaming windows, while the organ reverberates through the *close* and the silver treble of the boy choristers pierces the frosty air.

XVI

LITTLE PANTHEON OF THE THEATRE

THE Little Church Around the Corner had become the actors' place of worship by the merest chance back in the '70's, but their interest in it did not abate as time went on. After a few of its stage memorials had been installed it came to be known as the Little Pantheon of the Theatre, where the ecclesiastical and histrionic met in full accord. One of Dr. Ray's first thoughts on becoming rector was to crystallize this sentiment by means of an organization. His feeling for the theatre is one of his most characteristic qualities and, to-day, no clergyman can count as many actors and actresses among his friends as Dr. Ray. He knows them all and is a welcome figure at The Lambs and The Players. He will tell you that art is the handmaiden of the church and that the actor, with his emotional and artistic temperament, is inherently spiritual. He sincerely believes that there is true kinship between the pulpit and the stage, and he can offer proof from his own church, where the leading stars of five decades have worshipped, and the records are jammed with illustrious names of the theatre.

When the theatrical centre moved away from the vicinity of the church, and north to Times Square, the actors showed no fickleness where Transfiguration was concerned. In the days when Wallack, Mansfield and Montague were at the height of their powers, Twenty-ninth Street was the core of the night life. Daly's and Wallack's were only a step away from the church. But, as time went on, the theatre followed the irresistible flow of trade and crossed the old Thirty-fourth Street deadline. The change was swift and surprising to those who knew their New York. Charles Frohman was regarded as highly daring when he threw open the doors of the Empire Theatre at

Broadway and Fortieth Street, and Oscar Hammerstein was considered impractical when he built a theatre in the outlands north of Forty-second Street.

The sense of patronage and the social ostracism that had pursued the "play actor" disappeared along with the old theatres. The Actors' Church Alliance had flourished in Bishop Potter's time but, when the war came, it disintegrated, until there was little left but the name. Dr. Ray and the Rev. Walter E. Bentley tried to breathe life into the organization but they soon found that the day for it was past. There would have to be a fundamental change in the nature of the Alliance. Julia Marlowe, George Arliss and other stage stars were consulted and, after talking things over with them, Dr. Ray hit on the plan of forming the Guild. On a June afternoon in 1923 he held an informal gathering of actors and actresses, clergy and laity, and outlined his plan for a national body that would bring the theatrical profession and the church together for mutual welfare and entertainment. Mr. Arliss was elected president of the Guild, and Grant Mitchell, vice-president. For two years Dr. Ray gave his time personally to building it up. He succeeded in imparting vitality to the movement and in bringing the people of the stage into close contact with the church. From the beginning, the actors showed a responsive interest and the work progressed under the most favourable auspices. On February 24, 1924, the Guild Hall was opened in the dormer storey in the west wing of the church, with John Drew, Jane Cowl, John Emerson, Florence Reed and Otis Skinner among its sponsors. Bishop Manning was appointed honorary president and the advisory council was made up of a score of leading Episcopalian clergymen. For seven years Mr. Arliss has presided over the destinies of the Guild. In explaining its purposes he has said:

> The Episcopal Actors' Guild is not merely a sentimental alliance, not just a movement on the part of the church to show how broad-minded it is, not a gesture on the part of the actor to show how religious he is. It is a practical application of two distinct bodies which have greater power

in moulding public opinions and public morals than perhaps any medium in the world. Moreover, it has a very personal and practical side as is evidenced by the chain of active chapters from the Atlantic to the Pacific Ocean.

In no time at all the Guild was functioning on a national scale. It now has active chapters in forty cities and the membership has grown from a nucleus of a hundred to more than two thousand, with all the better known names of the theatre appearing on its roster, as well as a large church and lay following. Rexford Kendrick was the first secretary and Deaconess Jane H. Hall functioned as social director during its early days. As founder of the Three Arts Club, the Professional Children's School and the Rehearsal Club, she had unusual equipment, and her tact and intelligence did much to put it on a promising footing. Their work was successfully continued by Percy Moore and his assistant, Miss Katherine McEachern, who now may be found attending to the thousand and one activities that are directed behind the vine-covered lattice windows of the Guild Hall. The room is vast and lofty, with raftered ceiling and gabled roof. The little office, where all the correspondence and business affairs are handled, is three steps down through a grilled iron gate. In this setting Mr. Moore directs the national activities of the Guild, a connecting link between actors scattered all over the country. Few persons can claim as wide a theatrical acquaintance as Mr. Moore. He is an actor himself and understands the problems of those who seek aid from the Guild. He is a graduate of McGill University, Montreal, who turned from the study of medicine to the stage, appearing first before the footlights in 1901. He has played in Shakespeare, Shaw and many popular successes, and is a member of The Players and The Lambs. Mr. Moore has also produced several plays.

The Guild Hall is a genuine offspring of The Little Church Around the Corner, for it has the same sort of historic charm. A collection of Hollandia is being assembled in George Holland's desk, an old-fashioned affair with a glass-fronted top containing faded pictures and letters, with many allusions to Kate Holland, an actress of some note. The desk is the gift of Mrs. Charles

imp RLB

R L Boyer

GEORGE ARLISS
PRESIDENT OF THE ACTORS' GUILD

H. Tower, who felt that Transfiguration would be the most suitable setting for it when the actor's effects were being sold. Nearby is the pier mirror in which the beautiful Kate Claxton admired herself many years ago in her father's house on John Street. Brides sometimes don their veils and adjust their orange blossoms before it, with little thought of the actress of long ago who gave herself the finishing touches at this looking-glass. At the other end of the room is the heavy carved oak table that once belonged to Richard Mansfield, given by his wife, who still drops in for the Guild teas from time to time. On the plate is inscribed the actor's favourite line from Browning of one "who marched breast forward, never doubted clouds would break."

Old programmes and playbills, yellowing with the tinge of a romantic past, are hung around the room. They go back almost as far as the history of the church. First there is *Pique—A Play of To-day* at the Fifth Avenue Theatre, December 14, 1875—with Fanny Davenport, Mrs. G. H. Gilbert, Maurice Barrymore, John Drew and Kate Holland in the cast. And Joe Jefferson at the same theatre thirteen years later playing *The Rivals* with Mrs. John Drew and John Gilbert. A third bill from the same popular theatre recalls that Edwin Booth and Lawrence Barrett played there in November, 1888, in *The Merchant of Venice*. Jefferson is again billed in *The Cricket on the Hearth* at the Music Hall, 1886–87, where he also played the part of Caleb Plummer. Another programme dated 1887 announces the hundredth performance of *Jim the Penman* with E. M. Holland at the Madison Square Theatre. Old days in the theatre are further brought to mind with Augustin Daly's company playing *The Taming of the Shrew*, Edwin Booth and Lawrence Barrett in *The Merchant of Venice* and William Gillette in *Secret Service*, when it was new and thrilling, rather than a revival. The transition period from the '90's to the modern taste is typified by A. W. Pinero's *Sweet Lavender* produced at the Lyceum by Daniel Frohman, with Henry Miller and Mrs. Thomas Whiffen in the cast. Beside the office hangs a playbill announcing a testimonial tendered at Wallack's Theatre in 1901 to Mme. Fanny Janauschek by "The Women of the American

Stage," including the names of Julia Marlowe, Lillian Russell, Viola Allen, Blanche Bates and Amelia Bingham. Autographed pictures hang on the walls with the playbills. A coloured print of Ellen Terry as Mistress Page is autographed in her own neat script: "You are merry? So am I. Ha, ha."

Early in 1925 tableau curtains were installed in the Guild Hall so that it could be converted into a miniature theatre upon occasion. It has been put to this use frequently, for such diversified affairs as a drama of Chinatown, a farce, a musical comedy, an allegorical war play and a benefit performance for the Charlotte Cushman bust fund, when Edith Wynne Matthison, Amelia Bingham, H. Cooper Cliffe and other actors did scenes from Shakespeare in honour of a noted Lady Macbeth. The Guild Hall is open all the year round except for week-ends in summer, and generous use is made of these quarters. Here some of the church guilds assemble and it is not at all unusual at the meetings of the Altar Society to hear a young actress volunteer eagerly to clean the church silver or attend to the laces and vestments which are the especial care of this group. Dances, musical programmes, play discussions and a variety of special entertainments are held at regular intervals, and a benefit is staged for the Guild each November.

The teas are popular and here Broadway stars, who have long had their names twinkling in electric lights, chat over the tea-cups with admiring novices around a candle-lit table. Louise Closser Hale, Minnie Dupree or Ida Mulle, once a Broadway toast, may happen to be pouring tea, to the delight of the beginner. Mrs. Fiske, the Barrymores, Elsie Ferguson, Jane Cowl and Katherine Cornell are all enthusiastic members of the Guild, and one of its chief supporters is Percy Haswell (Mrs. George Fawcett), who founded the Guild council. Mrs. Channing Pollock, Mrs. Frank Gillmore and Mrs. Shelley Hull are regular tea hostesses, while Mrs. Edwina Booth Crossman and Mrs. Richard Mansfield, whose family names have been so closely associated with the church, drop in from time to time. Every producer and star of note is on the membership list and not a few take time to interest themselves actively in the work of the Guild. Young aspirants have received word of theatrical engagements over the tea table, and the stranger who has come to try her luck on Broadway has been given advice and sound social contacts. Two sisters who later became talented dancers haunted the Guild until they landed an engagement. They heard of an opening through someone they met there and before long they were headliners. One of them returned to the church to marry a young man to whom she had been introduced at a function in the Guild Hall.

The treasure chest of the Guild has outfitted many an actor with odds and ends needed for an engagement, and actresses who have been equipped to play in stock have later contributed articles of their own when their luck turned. All of the aid given is most informal. At times the Guild helps professionals in distress, caring for the sick and burying those who die without funds, but in no sense does it function as a charitable institution. All the relief work is subject to the approval of the Actors' Fund. Wherever the Guild has a chapter, its members are cared for, if they fall into difficulties. Eventually it is hoped that a rest house will be established in the country for ill or tired members of the profession, where they may be paying guests at a small weekly charge. If they are without means they will be carried along until they get on their feet again. It has always been one of Mr. Arliss's ideas to have a hostel for the children of professional people. He has seen this in successful operation in Great Britain and he believes that it would work here. But theatrical conditions have changed to such a degree that there is no longer the same need for it. Road companies have dwindled to nothing and stars do not find it necessary now to carry children across the continent and leave them in trunk lids in dressing rooms, as Kate Claxton had to do with her six infants in turn. Miss Hall, however, has taken a house in Montclair, N. J., opposite a good kindergarten, where she is taking care of a few stage children to see how much demand there is for a hostel of this sort.

The theatrical profession gave Dr. Ray a dinner at the Ritz-Carlton in May, 1930, in recognition of the work he had done for them during the first seven years of his incumbency. It was attended by two hundred of the leading producers and stars, and was presided over by Daniel Frohman. One after another, speakers rose to extol him and to express their affection for The Little Church Around the Corner. Virtually every one present had some sort of link with the actors' church, and had used its sacramental offices at one time or another. "You are my sort of people," said Dr. Ray, in acknowledging the compliments paid him. "I love the theatrical profession and the people in it, and I get my greatest satisfaction out of associating with you and ministering to you." With all its new memorials now installed, the actors on this occasion officially gave the church its third designation—The Little Pantheon of the Theatre.

XVII

IN MEMORIAM

ONE dull November day in 1925, when slate and purple shadows cast a smoky gloom over the city, Clara Morris lay in state in St. Joseph's Chapel, draped in a robe of pink silk, embroidered with blue butterflies. Six lighted candles, white and tall, were her footlights and, in their wavering light, a look of youth had returned to her face. Only her silver hair and clasped hands bore the imprint of age. Yet she was eighty, the star of a forgotten past. Crowded houses had once applauded her Camille and critics had said that it challenged Bernhardt herself. She had often come to The Little Church Around the Corner in her younger days and had been one of the leading figures in the testimonial for Holland.

Few people had seen her of recent years. Temporary blindness, illness and financial reverses had sent her into voluntary oblivion. But she maintained her sense of humour and, when a benefit was proposed for her, she addressed a jesting letter to Mr. Frohman:

> Is not Clara Morris pretty much of a legend now, a sort of Cinderella fable, based on that amazing Fifth Avenue opening night in 1875? Think of the years, think how the ranks of my beloved public have thinned. There are few who remember me now, I fancy—but oh, those few would remember vehemently with impetuosity of feeling! Such applause is the sweetest sound this side of heaven. I should love to hear it once more, but—(impersonal little word, always making trouble)—I have been outside of my house four times in eight years—rheumatism.

{ 127 }

But her funeral showed that she was still more than a legend. When the theatrical world learned that Clara Morris lay unnoticed, with a single knot of orchids by way of tribute for one who had once been handed sheaves of flowers across the footlights, they rallied around her and among those who filed past her bier in the dim candle-light were Robert Mantell, George Arliss, Gertrude Elliott and Grace Griswold. Grey-haired men and women who had played with her a generation before, and others who had tossed flowers to a great Camille, were among those who filled the church for the services. The pallbearers who walked behind her coffin, which was now covered with pink chrysanthemums and autumn leaves, were John Drew, Otis Skinner, David Warfield, Thomas Meighan, Frank Gillmore and Frederick Lewis. A strange little group hobnobbed in the churchyard after the services. Zadee Burbank, who had played with Miss Morris twenty-five years earlier at the conservative Lyceum, compared notes with Ella Lang, a *protégée* of the star, who had been a minor figure with her on the road in *Camille*. John R. Rogers, now feeble and old, recalled that he was so enthusiastic over Clara's acting back in the '60's, that he had induced the manager of Barney Macauley's stock theatre in Cincinnati to engage her. She played there for $40 a week until Augustin Daly signed her up at $250 a week. She appeared in stock under his wing at the Fifth Avenue Theatre in the summer of 1870, playing in the same company as Fanny Davenport. Her characterization of the creole Cora in *L'Article 47* made her famous, and four years later she won fresh laurels with her Camille. Although not as beautiful as many of her contemporaries Miss Morris outdid them all when it came to pathos, and when she appeared in *East Lynne* rivers of tears flowed from the impressionable audiences of a pre-Ibsen age. It was her own wish that she should be buried in the pink silk robe with butterflies, a frivolous touch for her bier.

Only a few months earlier Kate Claxton had been buried from The Little Church Around the Corner. She was seventy-four years old but kept her high spirits up to the time of her death. Her life was strangely ill-starred, one tragedy after another crossing her tempestuous path until managers feared to employ her because of her proverbial ill-luck. She was born in the year that Transfiguration was opened and she made her first public appearance in 1870, about the time that it was being christened The Little Church Around the Corner. She played with Lotta Crabtree and later became a member of that great training school of the period—Daly's stock company. From there she went to A. M. Palmer's Union Square Theatre where, like Miss Morris, she induced the tears of the Victorian age to flow over her tragic portrayal of the blind girl in *The Two Orphans*.

Miss Claxton was the heroine of the Brooklyn fire of 1876 and was burned in making her escape from the theatre. She went through several fires later on, one at a hotel in which she was living, another in her apartment, and a third in a theatre. She was married to Charles A. Stevenson, who played opposite Mrs. Leslie Carter in *Zaza*, but they were divorced in later years. Miss Claxton had six children, and many times she sat up all night on the train with a baby in each arm when she was touring from town to town. Years later her only son, considering himself a failure in life, committed suicide, adding another one to the innumerable Claxton misfortunes. She was a friend of The Little Church Around the Corner and sometimes sought Dr. Houghton's advice when her difficulties seemed overwhelming. She developed a philosophy of her own after everything that could happen to her had taken its course.

> Every woman must keep busy. Keeping busy helps one
> to forget oneself and selfishness is the first step toward old
> age. Don't brood. Live in the present. Live in the heart of
> a city. Keep busy. Laugh every day.

Amelia Bingham had seen the curtain fall on many of her contemporaries and had attended one funeral after another at The Little Church Around the Corner, as the stars of her generation passed on. In September, 1927, it was her turn, and again the chapel was banked with autumn flowers for a loved and accomplished player. The same faces filled the church, with perhaps a greater number of young people, moderns who had seen her play but were not old enough to remember Clara Morris and Kate Claxton. Grace Griswold's funeral was in June of the same year and several brides took their wedding vows in the church on the day that this star of the past was buried from Transfiguration. She had made her stage début with Daly in 1894 and had created the leading rôle in *A Burglar's Reception*. Her perennial part was in *Mrs. Wiggs of the Cabbage Patch*. Miss Griswold was more than casually interested in the church. She was the first secretary of the Actors' Church Alliance and founded the Charlotte Cushman Club of Philadelphia. She believed in the idea of the theatre workshop and helped to promote the association of church and drama.

Maurice Barrymore, father of Ethel, John and Lionel, and for years a distinguished figure on the stage, was buried from Transfiguration early in the century. He belonged to the era of Booth and Jefferson, playing with the latter in *The Rivals*. He was leading man with Modjeska and Mrs. Lily Langtry, and was a marvellous Rawdon Crawley opposite Mrs. Fiske in *Vanity Fair*. When Robert C. Hilliard, Broadway's Beau Brummell of the '90's, died at seventy years of age, he, too, was buried from the actors' church. On a June day in 1927 his coffin was borne down the aisle and *Crossing the Bar* was repeated once again for the passing of a figure luminous in the last century. William Courtleigh, who played the Friend to Hilliard's Husband in the morality thriller *A Fool There Was*, was an honorary pallbearer, and more than four hundred actors and actresses, representing many pages from the theatrical history of the past and present, were at the funeral. Plenty of them remembered the handsome, swashbuckling Bob Hilliard who had won the title in 1890 of the "handsomest man on the American stage," at a time when there were plenty of competitors for the supremacy which now goes to the crooners and the leading men of the cinema. Many a girl's heart had fluttered, watching handsome Bob in *Girl of the Golden West*, *Pride of the Race* and *The Argyle Case*. Among other actors buried from The Little Church Around the Corner in this century have been Henry Miller, James K. Hackett, James W. Wallack, Kyrle Bellew, Wallace Eddinger, Tom

Wise, Dustin Farnum, Walter Wilson, Grant Stewart, Charles A. Stevenson (the husband of Kate Claxton), Sidney Drew and Vernon Castle.

Sportsmen, writers, physicians and all manner of men have taken their last journey through the lich-gate. Leaders of the medical profession filed into the pews for the funeral of Dr. William E. Studdiford in November, 1925. He had been an attendant at Transfiguration for years, and his wife still worships there. In the following May, Francis R. Hitchcock, sportsman and steward of the Jockey Club for many years, was brought to the church for burial. He had died at sea on the *Olympic*, returning from France, where his racing colours were well known on the turf. The Hitchcocks had lived in the neighbourhood for many years and had had a deep attachment for the church. His father, Thomas Hitchcock, was buried there in 1910, the first of the Hitchcocks to foster the polo-playing tradition of the family in this country. One of the most unusual funerals in the history of the church was that of Miller Huggins in September, 1929, when a crowd of 10,000 pushed and elbowed its way around the iron fence to see Babe Ruth, Gehrig, Pennock, Shawkey and the other baseball idols who acted as pallbearers. Ruth wept like a child throughout the services for his late chief.

The Jefferson memorial window, one of the largest in the church, was unveiled and dedicated on the ninety-sixth anniversary of the actor's birth, February 20, 1925. John Drew was still alive and he delivered the eulogy, recalling that he had played with Jefferson in *Rip Van Winkle* when he was a young man being broken in to the stage tradition of his family. Charles A. Stevenson, who had known both Jefferson and Holland, also recalled his association with the famous actor. The window was unveiled by Miss Lauretta Jefferson Corlett, great-grand-daughter of Jefferson. Wambold's song *The Little Church Around the Corner* was sung and Jefferson's own poem *Immortality*, which President Grover Cleveland always referred to as the "butterfly poem," was recited. When Jefferson was in a sufficiently doleful mood on his fishing expeditions at Buzzard's Bay with President Cleveland, Richard Watson Gilder and, occasionally, Edwin Booth, he would repeat the poem. Copies of it were handed out at The Little Church Around the Corner at the memorial services held for him at the time of his death.

The theme of the Jefferson window is the parable of the Good Samaritan. It illustrates the story of the christening of The Little Church Around the Corner. Jefferson is shown in his tattered brown leather costume as the awakened Rip Van Winkle, supporting his actor friend, George Holland, who is wrapped in a shroud. They are met at the lich-gate by the Saviour, who stands with outstretched arms to welcome them. Below, on the scroll, are the words ascribed to Jefferson in response to Mr. Sabine's rebuff: "God Bless the Little Church Around the Corner." The insets portray scenes from the story of Rip Van Winkle. They represent his wife scolding him as he idles with his dog, and the long draught of wine which sends him to sleep for twenty years, and his horror as he awakens in the Catskills in rags, and wonders what has happened. Hendrik Hudson's men are shown drinking from great steins and playing ninepins, a scene which caused some comment when it first made its appearance in the church. Walter Wilson, the actor, who was later buried from Transfiguration, suggested the various scenes and the central theme of the window.

John Drew, who had been deeply attached to the church, died in July, 1927, while playing in San Francisco in a revival of *Trelawney of the Wells*. A memorial service was held for him and, more than a year later, actors famous a generation ago and stars of the present day assembled at the church for the dedication of his memorial window. It faces the Jefferson memorial and was unveiled by John Drew Devereux, Drew's only grandchild, while Miss Ethel Barrymore and Mr. and Mrs. Jack Devereux, the donors, looked on. The memorial is Gothic and the chief figure is St. John the Evangelist, with minor figures representing Love, Faith and Hope. Walter Hampden, Frank Gillmore and Daniel Frohman, whose brother Charles was John Drew's manager for many years, all made addresses. The actor's links with the church were numerous. He was married, and his daughter, Louise, was baptized in it. After her death he sent lilies every Easter for the altar in memory of his wife. He attended the funerals and weddings of countless friends there as the years went on. He had played with Booth in *Hamlet* and with Jefferson in *Rip Van Winkle*. He was leading juvenile with Fanny Davenport, and many of those who attended his funeral remembered the night of April 13, 1887, when Drew, Ada Rehan and Mrs. Gilbert, who was also buried from the church, were celebrating their hundredth performance in *The Taming of the Shrew* at Daly's. The gaslight sputtered on the dusty red plush boxes and the house with filled with the beaux and belles of the day. Sarah Bernhardt was playing *Theodora* and Patti was singing at the Metropolitan. *The Black Crook* was going strong at Niblo's.

In the spring of 1930 two other memorials were unveiled in the church, one to Mary Shaw, actress and feminist; the other in honour of all actors and actresses. Miss Shaw's window was the gift of the Gamut Club, an organization for professional women which she had founded, and of which she was president up to the time of her death. The window was dedicated by Dr. Ray and was unveiled by Mrs. Adelaide Shaw, a sister of the actress. Its three oval panes illustrate scenes from the life of St. Ursula, patron saint of educational institutions for women. Prominent feminists as well as stage people filled the church on this occasion.

Transfiguration was packed on the March day on which Kathryna Ray unveiled the window over the transept which is inscribed: "In honour of all actors and actresses who for the love of Christ have served." It is, in effect, a memorial to the unknown actor and was designed and given to the church by Miss Jessie Van Brunt. The theme of the window is the flight into Egypt and here again an unusual effect is achieved in the church, for it is done in the modern manner, a vivid desert scene with camels and waving palm trees, lotus blossom and the papyrus plant. In presenting the window Miss Van Brunt explained its purpose:

> Many of our greatest actors and actresses have no public memorial, as well as some of the loyal members of the profession who have given their best to their beloved art

and have passed on, forgotten, perhaps, beyond their own generation of admirers. To all these, this window is gratefully dedicated, for all have given their gifts freely to serve their public and the world of culture and art.

In May, 1928, Mrs. Strombom died at her home in Bedford Village and was buried from the church where she had been active for many years. Her body lay in state in the Lady Chapel, her father's memorial to her mother. In the following March a brilliant clerestory window was dedicated in her honour. In selecting this window, Dr. Ray took care to choose vivid blues, green and reds, as more suitable to her character than tepid pastel shades. The window is the gift of her close friends, and faces down the transept near the pulpit on the north side, where her father used to preach. The theme is symbolic to some degree of Mrs. Strombom's life. It shows Dorcas distributing clothes and food; St. Elizabeth with her lap filled with roses; St. Catherine with her wheel and palm of martyrdom; and St. Agnes with her lamb and palm. Dominating the design are the Blessed Virgin and Child. Beneath the window is a bronze tablet bearing the Houghton coat-of-arms.

XVIII

ORANGE BLOSSOMS

FAR above all its other claims to fame, Transfiguration is the church
of brides. In thousands they have knelt at its altar, the lovely and the plain;
the simple, cynical, sophisticated and romantic; the stage star, business girl
and débutante; the young and the middle-aged. They have been married in
sunshine and in rain, when the fountain was frozen in icy stalactites and on
warm June days when it played a rippling accompaniment to the Wedding
March. They have taken their marriage vows in spring when the daffodils
nodded in golden rows, and in autumn when the leaves drifted from the elms
and whirled in the path of the bridal party. Styles in wedding frocks and
bouquets have changed with the passing years. Taste in rings has evolved
from thick gold hoops to wafer-like circlets of platinum, from crescents of
diamonds to the solitaire or baguette, but the aura of romance has remained
unchanged at The Little Church Around the Corner.

First the brides came to the founder of the church, saintly and kind, who
beamed on them and wished them luck. Then they came to the second Dr.
Houghton, sterner in his requirements but cordial as he urged them to be
good mates. Now they come to Dr. Ray, who starts them on their way with
whatever good wishes spring spontaneously to mind after he has pronounced
them man and wife. Although the wedding parties move through the church
with the ceaselessness of an advancing army, and one bride follows another
into the little office with her flowers and bridesmaids, there is never an air
of hurry as young couples kneel before the brides' altar. Here sentiment has
a permanent lodging place, and the odour of orange blossoms lingers with a
haunting fragrance night and day. Lohengrin ushers them in and they leave

{ 135 }

the altar to the strains of Mendelssohn's Wedding March. It has been found at The Little Church Around the Corner that the modern bride is quite as serious as her ancestors in her approach to the wedding ceremony and all flippancies are dropped when she walks through the lich-gate. The changing mode has been superficial—a matter of frocks, rings, flowers, first names and the disappearance of *obey* from the wedding service.

The early brides to take their vows at Transfiguration, contemporaries of Serena Keeler, wore their hair flat over their ears, had round *décolletages* and bridal veils that stopped short of the hem of their tiered crinolines. Their names were apt to be of the old-fashioned order, like Fanny, Laura, Agatha, Emily, or Sue. By 1860 the crinolines were more exuberant, but bows and puffs had taken the place of tiers, and the bridesmaids wore Quaker bonnets with wide ribbons knotted under their chins. Rows of heavy embroidery embellished their billowing frocks. By 1870, when some of New York's smartest damsels were getting married in the church, the crinoline had surrendered to the bustle, and haughty brides rustled down the aisle with tassels, pointed basques and veils that were gathered high in a peak and tumbled in heavy cascades to the ankle. The bridesmaids wore fringed or beaded tippets, Victorian bonnets tied under the chin, and impressive bustles.

By 1880 waists were at their slimmest and frills had reached their zenith, so that the bride was lost in ruffles and clouds of lace. Her hair was done in the waterfall mode. Her attendants had hourglass figures, hats that had abandoned their chin straps but were still of the Quaker family, and ruchings of braid that swept the floor. By 1890 Dr. Houghton, now old and feeble, ministered to young ladies severely attired in moulded frocks with high, stiff collars and long satin trains. The veil fell heavily from a mound of orange blossom on top of a fringed coiffure. Bridesmaids ran to dark silk frocks with voluminous skirts, and to the first manifestation of the picture hat, poised on the back of the head and springing upwards with an ostrich tip or two.

When the second Dr. Houghton was beginning his long history as the "marrying parson" at the opening of the century, the brides who passed before him were stately and ran to curves. They had tucked bodices, neat waists and full, gored skirts. They carried round nosegays with frilled borders and their bridal veils hung from the first of the pompadours, for the Gibson girl was in vogue. By 1910 curves were still in the mode but tunics and panels were simplifying the bridal frocks. Long gloves were worn with short sleeves and the veil hung from a mob-cap of tulle and orange blossom. In 1920 the hobble skirt was having its brief day and bouquets had grown to fancy proportions. In 1925 Dr. Ray was marrying flappers who had achieved a neat but abbreviated wedding frock, and to-day he is ministering to brides with long skirts, the normal waistline and a pronounced throw-back to some of the earlier fashions of The Little Church Around the Corner.

In June the formal weddings are at their height, and girls in satin, tulle and orange blossom, kneel at the chancel rail in the church, or else before the shining altar of blue and gold which is their especial possession in the Chapel of the Holy Family. But most of the marriages are informal, the brides usually wearing lace or chiffon frocks with horsehair or leghorn hats. Orchids and lilies-of-the-valley have supplanted the lily as the favourite wedding flower at the church of brides. Dr. Ray finds that the modern girl is apt to prefer a quiet ceremony in the presence of a few relatives and friends, and a number of débutantes who have had elaborate weddings planned for them have slipped quietly in to Transfiguration to avoid all fuss and still be married in surroundings both churchly and picturesque. Personally Dr. Ray likes to see a bride in traditional attire and he has a weakness for the old-fashioned wedding ring. When he sees a hoop of gold being produced he always looks with interest at the bride, expecting to find a woman of independence and intellect who also has a strain of sentiment.

Each June brings its rush of brides to the church, with 349 weddings in June, 1929, and 305 in June, 1930. August and September come next in popularity, and April ranks fourth with its Easter brides, who have lilies on the altar and lilies for their bouquets. December is fifth on the list and usually rates 200 weddings. The Little Church Around the Corner is never lovelier than under snow, and the brides who take their wedding vows at Christmas time kneel in a setting of holly, mistletoe and evergreens. May and November, the month of requiem, are traditionally unpopular for weddings, but the superstition must be almost outgrown, for both have rated high in the wedding statistics of recent years. November challenges lucky April and in May the average is steadily rising.

The marriage tradition of the church grew up almost imperceptibly. The first bride's life was a happy one, and fifty-four of her descendants have watched Transfiguration's history with affectionate interest. Serena's father, Matthew Keeler, came to Dr. Houghton's parish from St. Bartholomew's, where he had sung bass in the choir. One girl who was to have preceded her died in the spring, so that it was Serena's lot to be the first to take her vows at the altar of the brides' church. A year later Elizabeth Eyland was baptized in the church, the first of eleven children. Many branches grew from this family tree. There were twenty-four grandchildren, eighteen great-grand-children, and recently a great-great-grandchild of Serena's was born. Three years after their marriage the Eylands moved to New Jersey but, when the first child grew up and married Randall C. Hall, Professor of Hebrew at the General Theological Seminary, she attended Transfiguration again and was buried from there not long ago. Her son, Serena's youngest grandchild, was married in the church in 1926.

The records show that it was four months before Dr. Houghton was called on to perform another wedding ceremony. In fact, there were only twenty-five in the first three years of his ministry, and the number of weddings for the first twenty years equals the figures for a month at the present time. But the '70's saw a big increase. The Holland episode had attracted public attention, and theatrical marriages had become so numerous that visitors from abroad and from all parts of the United States sought out Joe Jefferson's church as a matter of curiosity. By the close of the century the wedding statistics were running into four figures and, during his first five years at Transfiguration, the second Dr. Houghton married nearly 10,000 couples.

A new peak was reached under **Dr. Ray** when 2,346 couples were married in 1930. Many of the applicants are sentimental enough to believe that they may avert divorce by starting with the blessing of the church that has acquired one tradition after another of good luck and romance. As a matter of fact, it is a point of pride with Dr. Ray that the average number of successful marriages seems to be high. An impending divorce always comes to the attention of the rector through the lawyer's application for a certificate to accompany the papers filed in the divorce court. The number of requests of this nature would indicate that about eighty-five per cent of the marriages solemnized at The Little Church Around the Corner endure.

It is not unusual for as many as a thousand couples to be turned away in a year and among them have been celebrities who have been both surprised and chagrined to find divorce an insuperable barrier. Dr. Ray explains that his stand is purely orthodox and is founded on the canon of the Episcopal Church—Matthew 19:6: "What therefore God hath joined together, let not man put asunder." With the increase in divorce the situation has become sufficiently embarrassing for the church to seek the co-operation of the Marriage License Bureau. The clerks watch for marriage license applications on which a previous divorce is recorded, and they warn the pair of the situation at The Little Church Around the Corner. The rules are rigid:

> *All divorced persons are barred*
> *Applicants must be baptized*
> *Parents or guardians must be informed of the marriage*

Once the questionnaire has been filled in, special emphasis is placed on the formal vow of the applicant:

> *We, the undersigned, solemnly swear without evasion or reservation, that the above statements are true, that we are not divorced, that our parents or guardians are aware of this marriage, that we are of legal age, that there is no impediment or objection to our marriage, and that we are entering it of our own free will.*

Sometimes it is found that a youthful applicant lies about an elopement, as in the case of the girl who swore that the man who sponsored her, when she married a boy of her own age, was her uncle. It turned out that he was the captain of her father's yacht and she had persuaded him to aid and abet her in a runaway marriage. Occasionally they write in later to announce that they have fooled the vigilants at The Little Church Around the Corner. They like to point out that the marriage has been a happy one and, in this event, they explain their secrecy in great detail. There is less rushing in to be married at a moment's notice now than there used to be. Through constant repetition the idea has spread that it is advisable to make arrangements well in advance. The church is so much in demand for weddings that this has become almost a necessity, if one bride is not to jostle another. As it is, the bridesmaids of different wedding parties are often mixed like a bouquet of assorted flowers in the *close* and there is no time to sweep up the confetti between one ceremony and the next.

Dr. Ray is a stickler as a clergyman on the subject of marriage. He believes that the sacrament has not changed during the Christian era and the only kind of union he recognizes, in so far as his ministration in the church is concerned, is the "old-fashioned marriage." Yet his feeling does not extend to his social relations. He is warm friends with stage people who have had a number of divorces, and this is typical of the blend of toleration and church form that has always prevailed at Transfiguration. They are welcome to any of the other offices of the church. He has frequently enunciated his own convictions on marriage.

> No matter how many substitutes may be tried, how many theories proposed, there is only one permanent normal relationship upon which a home can be established and that is the relationship of one man and one woman joined together at God's altar for better or for worse until death do them part. Marriage has not changed since the Christian era. The only kind of marriage I know about is the old-fashioned kind.

imp RLB   R L Boyer

BRIDES' CHAPEL

Dr. Ray marvels that so many marriages turn out well. He believes that if men and women pursued their business and artistic careers as carelessly as they do their married life, and trusted as haphazardly to luck, the results would be disastrous nine times out of ten. The altar in the Chapel of the Holy Family testifies to the fact that many of the brides of The Little Church Around the Corner have lived happily ever after, for it was given by those whose names are now inscribed in a red leather book kept in a compartment inside the railing. It was dedicated in October, 1926, and is a memorial to the second Dr. Houghton. The altar is of mellow-toned Botticino marble imported from Italy, with an inlay of French Tavernelle. The tabernacle door glitters with diamonds, sapphires, rubies, amethysts, garnets and other precious stones given by brides from their own jewel boxes, an enduring evidence of their affection. The gems are from engagement rings or from family heirlooms, and they all represent some affectionate association with the church.

The reredos achieves a glamorous effect, with its rich transfusion of colour. The triptych is done in gold, blue, green and a soft, dark red that repeats the tones of the stained glass windows along the wall. A pierced frieze of Ascension lilies surrounds it, and adoring angels are painted in colours and gold on the outer doors. When closed it shows a Latin cross with a halo, enclosed in a Gothic arch. A painting on wood represents *The Betrothal of the Blessed Virgin* with three figures—a high priest in rich vestments between the Virgin and St. Joseph. Inset, in the central panel beneath these figures, is the worm-eaten and priceless carving of black oak which is more than four hundred years old and was taken from a dismantled monastery in the Highlands of Scotland. It is a memorial to Miss Jennie W. McComb and was the gift of her niece, Miss Madge McComb. The old Scottish superstition of good luck attends this carving of three Crucifixion scenes, and many brides who have heard about it examine the historic possession while they are in the Chapel of the Holy Family. Carved figures of the Four Evangelists rest in niches around the central panels. The altar rail, before which the brides kneel, is the gift of E. F. Albee, who was a patron of the Actors' Guild during his later years. The reredos was given by friends and parishioners. Over the spot where Dr. Ray joins the hands of bride and groom with his twisted stole hangs an old silver lamp given by Mrs. Harold F. Hadden. It has a Russian crucifix embedded in the melted silver and looks like a reversed Roman helmet, adding another unusual touch to a unique bridal chapel. The first wedding solemnized before the new altar was a theatrical one, Lyons Wickland marrying Grace Cecile Hatch, a Dallas girl. One step from the altar is the old font with brass filigree, where brides of the church prefer to have their babies baptized. And, through its stained glass sliding doors, may be glimpsed the marble purity of the Lady Chapel, like an alabaster vase in a dark oak setting.

XIX

A CALENDAR OF BRIDES

FAMOUS as well as lovely have been many of the brides of The Little Church Around the Corner, and Irene Castle and Ann Harding still rank in the forefront of the well-known beauties who have been married there. Visitors who pause in the church to watch a stage wedding may see a dozen stars assembled at one time in the straight oak pews of the Chapel of the Holy Family, for Broadway has a well-worn path to the altar of Joe Jefferson's church. Delicate as an orchid, with her spun-gold hair and creamy pallor, Miss Harding knelt beside Harry C. Bannister before the gilded reredos on an October afternoon in 1926. They were both appearing in plays on Broadway at the time.

Charlie Chaplin and Douglas Fairbanks were ushers when Robert E. Sherwood was married in 1922 to Mary Brandon, an actress and niece of Booth Tarkington. Mary Pickford beamed on the bride and groom from an aisle seat and the church was filled with stage, cinema and literary celebrities. Baird Leonard walked down the aisle with Harry St. Clair Zogbaum three months after Ann Harding was married. Appropriately enough, the great grand-daughter of Joe Jefferson took her wedding vows in November, 1929, with the son of Jefferson's leading lady of long ago. The girl was Cynthia Carol Corlett, and the bridegroom was Edwin Ogden Childe, whose mother, Mrs. Alberta Childe, was a toasted actress in the days of the coach and four. Three other grand-daughters of Joe Jefferson were present—Mrs. Charles H. Raymond, Mrs. Rumsey Wing Scott and Mrs. Carrington Howard. And one of the first persons to kiss the bride was Fred Ross, an aged actor-manager who played with Jefferson and Booth in those distant days when actors were married and buried with little ceremony.

A number of George Holland's descendants have sought the offices of the church, keeping the historic connection alive. His grandchildren and his great-grandchildren have been baptized at the old font, and in 1918 Joseph Edmund William Holland, son of Joseph Holland 2d, was married to Julieena Jessay. The tradition of the stage marriage, which is one of the distinguishing features of The Little Church Around the Corner to-day, was well established in the time of the founder. Arthur, the son of Lester Wallack, was married by him in 1881, the year the surpliced choir was installed. In the following year Marion Caroline Davenport, of the famous theatrical family of that name, took her wedding vows at Transfiguration. David S. Wambold, who wrote the minstrel song that was to carry the fame of the church far and wide, chose to be married at its altar in the summer of 1880. Holbrook Blinn was one of the many stage celebrities married there during the '90's. Various branches of the Drew family have figured in the church records for three decades, and Mr. and Mrs. Sidney Drew were married in 1914 by the second Dr. Houghton.

John E. Hazzard was another of the stage bridegrooms of The Little Church Around the Corner, and Grace Norma White was married there to "Poodles" Hanneford, one of the five equestrian stars of the same name who flourished in the palmy days of the Hippodrome. This was a romance of the ring. Miss White was in a cycling act and was wooed by the horseback clown. It is a matter of course at The Little Church Around the Corner for babies and grand-children to be brought back for baptism and confirmation. Little David Weaver, the child of Peggy Wood and John V. A. Weaver, was baptized there in December, 1927, the Rev. Dr. James V. Huntington officiating. King Constantine of Greece was sponsor by proxy for Jean Constantine Hibben, the daughter of Paxton Hibben. The child was baptized in the winter of 1922 and Bishop Gemamos of the Greek Church represented King Constantine. Mr. Hibben is the author of *Constantine I and the Greek People*. This was one of the most ceremonious baptisms in the history of the church.

The records of Transfiguration are almost as liberally sprinkled with the names of artists, writers and musicians as with actors. Paderewski was a witness at the wedding of a Polish violinist on one occasion, and all the arts have been represented at different times. Howard Chandler Christy's daughter, Nathalie, was baptized in the church, and James Montgomery Flagg was married there in 1924. His parents, Mr. and Mrs. Elisha Flagg, had been married by Dr. Houghton many years before, and in 1925 his daughter was brought to the font for baptism and was named Faith Flagg, a typical example of the perpetuated tradition of The Little Church Around the Corner. Rollin Kirby was married by Dr. Houghton in the early part of the century at about the same time that a young Canadian named Stephen Leacock, who had not yet attained notice in *belles-lettres*, walked in to take his marriage vows. Mary Jane Outcault, the heroine of the Buster Brown cartoons and the daughter of Richard F. Outcault, the cartoonist who created them, was married in 1921 to Frank Edwin Pershing, a nephew of General John J. Pershing. Mary Jane is numbered among the youngest and most widely known brides of the church, for the doings of her childhood have been fully recorded in the Buster Brown strip.

A débutante of international reputation sought the offices of The Little Church Around the Corner on June 28, 1927, after going through a civil ceremony at the Municipal Building earlier in the day. Miss Grace Vanderbilt surprised her parents, General and Mrs. Cornelius Vanderbilt, by marrying Henry Gassaway Davis 3d without any preliminary announcement. A traffic policeman and Colonel Henry Howell Armstead, uncle of the bridegroom, were the witnesses at the civil ceremony. In the meantime Mrs. Davis had sent a note to her parents, announcing what she had done and suggesting a church marriage. The young couple waited all day for some word from the Vanderbilts but none came. At 11 o'clock at night they decided they would go to The Little Church Around the Corner. Dr. Ray was out and, in his absence, the Rev. Culver B. Alford was hesitant about performing the ceremony. The fact that they were already married under the law made the church sacrament possible, even under the strictest interpretation of the canons. Yet it was clearly an elopement. The young pair decided to wait until the last minute, on the chance that Dr. Ray might come in. At 11.50 o'clock they persuaded the priest to officiate and they were married in the brides' chapel just before midnight, with Colonel Armstead again serving as a witness, this time along with a night watchman, Edward Owen.

Grace Vanderbilt was not the first member of her family to be married in Transfiguration. Towards the close of the nineteenth century Alice Vanderbilt Shephard and David H. Morris were married by the founder of the church. The bride's parents, Mr. and Mrs. Elliott Fitch Shephard, were members of the parish. Before her marriage Mrs. Shephard was Margaret Louisa Vanderbilt, sister of the elder Mrs. Cornelius Vanderbilt. During the '80's and '90's several branches of the family attended the church.

For twenty years Dr. Ray had known Miss Evangeline Adams and she had read his horoscope on different occasions, so that when she decided to marry George Edwin Jordan, whose horoscope was in full accord with hers, she came to Transfiguration for the ceremony. Miss Adams's assorted following filled the church, deeply interested in the outcome of a wedding arranged correctly according to the stars. Another of the more unusual weddings at the church was the re-marriage of Mr. and Mrs. Morton H. Hoyt on Christmas Eve, 1928, a reconciliation that did not last. Mrs. Hoyt was formerly Eugenia Bankhead, sister of Tallulah Bankhead. Mr. Hoyt was the brother of Elinor Wiley and the son of Henry M. Hoyt, Solicitor-General during the Taft administration. They were married for the first time at Bar Harbor in 1920 and were divorced in Reno eight years later. Within less than a year they had decided to marry again and they came to Transfiguration. A notation in the church records describes it as a "reconciliation service because of certain religious rules regarding the marriage of divorced persons." So far as the Anglican communion was concerned they had never been divorced, and Dr. Ray saw no impropriety in a second solemnization. They used their old wedding ring for the second service.

ПОР RLB   R L Boyer

THE LADY CHAPEL

No matter how modern the bride, wedding rings still figure prominently in the arrangements, and Miss Hanlon is a vigilant duenna who sees that absent-minded and nervous bridegrooms do not mislay the small hoop of platinum or gold and hold up the responses. But now and again the ring is lost, and embarrassing scenes ensue. One of the favourite ring stories dates back to the time of the second Dr. Houghton and involves an anxious bridegroom who pinned the ring to his waistcoat and made much ado about it when he came to make the preliminary arrangements. He was singularly proud of the chased platinum ring set with diamonds, a fashion that was just coming in, and he produced the white kid bag from his vest pocket to dazzle Miss Hanlon.

"Very nice!" commented that wise observer of grooms and brides. "But take care you don't lose it."

"Trust me for that," he reassured her, exhibiting a safety pin that fastened the bag to his pocket.

On the day before the wedding he was back again making final arrangements. Passing the secretary's desk he patted his pocket to show her that all was well. But the next day the bridal party was ready to file into the church when the bridegroom turned grey and gasped as he pressed his chest. He had changed his business suit for formal wedding attire and the ring was still safely clamped to the pocket of the discarded waistcoat. Someone present produced a ring that had already done service, and the new one was brought back later to be blessed at the altar. The experienced observers at the brides' church find that the girl is invariably less flustered than the man on these occasions and can usually be counted upon to meet emergencies without undue embarrassment. While most of the brides come with their attendants and all their wedding finery already in place, others borrow a room in the rectory or Guild Hall in which to change, and also ask for witnesses, if they happen to be strangers in town. There are several cases where girls have come all the way across the continent just to be married in The Little Church Around the Corner. A San Franciscan who was educated in the East had her heart set on being married there. The bridegroom was a California state senator. They brought their parents with them and had as formal a wedding as if the church were filled with guests. The girl wore the lace veil that had been used by several generations of brides in her family. At eight o'clock in the evening she went up to the Guild Hall and adjusted her veil and wedding dress before Kate Claxton's mirror. None of their friends was in the city but they went through the full ceremonial, in the presence of their parents, with music, flowers, and lighted candles. This was devotion to a remembered picture of the interior of The Little Church Around the Corner! Another couple came from Vancouver to be married, but they engaged a private railroad car and brought cousins, aunts and friends along with them, so that the chantry was well filled when they walked up to the altar.

Romance has been shadowed at times by tragedy, tears and crime, an unavoidably muddy reflection in the limpid serenity of a church touched by strong currents of life. Shortly after the Armistice a handsome pair came in to be married and there seemed to be no impediments in their way. He was an English army officer, she an American ambulance driver. They were unaccompanied and were taken upstairs to the oratory, where Dr. Houghton frequently tied the nuptial knot when there were no guests or attendants. As usual, he told them to be good mates and the bride, hearing his words, walked over to the window and burst into tears. Dr. Houghton was surprised; the bridegroom even more so. He said that he had seen her under fire but had never known her to weep.

They went out after she had regained her self-control and the sequel to the story was soon heard at the church. A week later a United States army officer walked in. He was a man of about fifty, tall and stiff in his bearing. He produced a framed photograph and asked the secretary if she could remember having seen the original. Miss Hanlon realized at once that she was looking at the face of the woman who had broken down after being married. The visitor explained that she was his wife and that she had not let him know that she was back from Europe. He looked over the wedding certificate, a painful ordeal, for his fears were confirmed. The proofs of bigamy were before him. Her nerve had not held out. After leaving the church she had told the Englishman the truth. He had left her and notified her husband. The church of romance had no balm for a case of this sort.

On another occasion a fussy woman in her early forties came to the church to make arrangements for her wedding, announcing that she was a widow. Her behaviour was eccentric but little notice is taken of personal idiosyncrasy in the busy office of Transfiguration. She returned repeatedly to the church, making all sorts of demands. She wanted the altar decorated with lilies. A musician friend of hers was to play the Wedding March. She told of the guests who had been invited; of her frock, her veil and her orange blossoms. She explained that her first wedding had been meagre and she wanted this one to be ceremonious. On the night set for the ceremony rain lashed the church, the eaves dripped and thunder rolled over the city. The couple arrived in the midst of the downpour. In their dash through the *close*, the satin, tulle and orange blossoms were sadly wilted. None of the guests showed up, nor even the vaunted organist. The prospective bride and groom sat down in the empty church with the officiating priest and listened to the rain beating on the roof. The woman maintained the fiction as long as she could, nervously twitching at her veil and wondering audibly why no one came. At last the groom lost patience and said they would proceed with the ceremony—a melancholy affair with the bride on the verge of tears. Years later the riddle was solved. The woman was a bigamist. The husband returned eventually and told of his discovery, shortly after the wedding ceremony, that his supposed wife was supplying her first husband with the money he was giving her.

Death bed marriages have occasionally been performed by the rectors of Transfiguration and the emergencies of life have been met without question. The second Dr. Houghton risked a breach of the civil law in order to marry a girl whose baby was about to be born. The man was a soldier and he was sailing for overseas on the night that they came to the church, accompanied by the girl's parents. They had no marriage license and the bureau was closed for the day. After making repeated efforts to reach one of the clerks at his home Dr. Houghton announced that he would marry them if he had to go to jail or pay a fine. The ceremony was performed in the oratory, the secretary acting as a witness. The soldier had no ring and Dr. Houghton gave him one he had bought years earlier in London. He reported what he had done to the Marriage License Bureau next day. The District Attorney's office was informed but he heard no more about it. Many soldiers rushed in to be married at the last minute before going overseas. Some of them kissed their brides good-bye at the door and the girls returned to kneel in the quiet chantry and pray for their return. One soldier who is remembered well at the church kept repeating: "I *will* come back." The transport on which he went over was torpedoed and he was shockingly hurt but the vow he had made in the church to his wife held good and, eventually, he did come back. When last heard from they were living happily in Pennsylvania.

When a young American girl walked in to the office and announced that she wished to marry a Chinese, Miss Hanlon talked to her for an hour, pointing out the difficulties that would beset her path. But not long ago she had a letter from her written in Shanghai, saying that her marriage had been wonderfully happy and that the fears expressed at the church on her behalf were unfounded. Because of the informal manner in which many of its couples drop in to be married, various emergencies have to be met at The Little Church Around the Corner. On one occasion a canary chirped all through the ceremony from his perch in a pew. The girl had arrived with the bird in its cage, as she had just reached town and did not know where to leave it. No one was available to see that the canary was safe while the service was going on, so it was carried into the chantry and burst into trills of song as the Wedding March was played. Another time the church had evidently been made the subject of a dare, for, while a girl sat out at the gate in a carriage— long after the close of the carriage age—her companion came in and asked if he could bring his dog to the wedding. Dr. Ray thought not. Meanwhile, a

{150}

crowd on the street was being edified by a strange spectacle. An old-fashioned equipage with coachman and footman stood at the gate and in the back seat was a huge dog with a collar trimmed with flowers. It was plain that a hoax of some sort was being perpetrated. When the man came out, reporting that the dog could not be taken into the church, the carriage drove off. But that did not end the day's adventures.

A formal wedding was scheduled for later in the afternoon. The bride was late and Dr. Ray was in the middle of telling the bridegroom the story of the flower-decked dog when another young man popped in and said he wanted to be married. He, too, had a dog outside which he said he would like to bring in. It was only a lapdog this time and the waiting bridegroom volunteered to take charge of it while its owner got married. In they all marched to the chantry, forgetting that it was filled with guests waiting for the formal wedding. However, the assemblage showed no concern over witnessing two ceremonies instead of one. But this proved to be one of the unfortunate occasions when the bridegroom had mislaid the ring. He and his best man rustled through their pockets with the glassy look that usually accompanies this operation, while Dr. Ray waited patiently and the audience shuffled in embarrassed sympathy. Miss Hanlon found the ring eventually in the pocket of a coat that had been left outside in the office.

Marriage licenses also have a way of being forgotten and not long ago a wedding was postponed for two hours while the essential document was brought in from Long Island. One of the most novel delays was occasioned by a bride's mother who held up the ceremony for forty minutes while she waited for a milliner to finish her hat. She was going to appear in that particular bonnet and none other. The reverse was true of the agitated bridegroom who arrived immaculately attired up to his chin but without any hat at all. A thoughtful friend came stalking him with his topper, so that he could leave the church in the mould of fashion.

There are times when laughter rocks the matrimonial bark at The Little Church Around the Corner.

XX

FAMILY OF THE LITTLE CHURCH

THE third bread line established by the Church of the Transfiguration brought a shuffling army of men who rubbed shoulders with satin-clad brides and doffed their ragged hats in courtly deference to romance. "God bless you" some of them murmured with watery eyes—Soapy's own brothers—as they edged along the queue and peered through the iron fence at the bridesmaids clustered around the newly married girl at the door. For 1930 was a year of strange contrasts at the church, as the unemployed besieged it and almost succeeded in swamping its other activities. The *close* echoed to the tramp of hungry suppliants and O. Henry characters crowded around the lich-gate seeking the literal bread of life.

Following the precedents of 1864 and 1907, the bread line was started in a modest way when it became apparent that unemployment was reaching serious proportions. Dr. Ray had no idea that his meal tickets would lead to a sensational queue that had to be curbed when it got out of hand and stretched up Madison Avenue to Thirtieth Street and west again in the direction of Fifth Avenue. More than 75,000 jobless and hungry men received aid within a few weeks' time. Interested in what he saw at the gates of The Little Church Around the Corner, Heywood Broun opened an employment bureau across the street and jobs were found for hundreds of the likeliest candidates. Only a step from one of the world's richest thoroughfares the starving and destitute clamoured for food and for work, a twentieth century anomaly that had no parallel in old New York.

The line began to form at the church as early as six o'clock in the morning, with the police keeping order. At first the tickets were distributed in the office, but this soon became impracticable as the queue grew to unwieldy proportions. It was then that Dr. Ray took up his stand under the lich-gate, dispensing charity with the aid of a curate and Harry Davenport, the actor. More than a thousand men would be in line four abreast by nine o'clock, and 1,840 were fed on the first of April. The loaves and fishes of Biblical tradition were matched by a twenty-cent meal of potatoes, beef stew and coffee. The tickets entitled the men to food at any one of four different eating places. They were grateful, sulky, responsive or cheerful, according to their dispositions. Some were professional hoboes from the Bowery, always on hand for a free meal; the majority were men out of work and in want. A post card received later by Dr. Ray gives an inkling of what some of them felt.

> May I not thank you in behalf of your immaculate church for relieving me of my ravenous hunger yesterday with a meal ticket? Surely you act on a literal obedience to the Scripture and be assured, reverend sir, when ability serves a generous retribution will be made. May the angels (sic) be ever your guardian is the prayer of a grateful friend.
>
> *George.*

Contributions poured in for the bread line and bridegrooms rarely passed the straggling ranks without digging their hands in their pockets to lessen another man's misery. Clothing and boots were provided, as well as food and work. Meanwhile, wedding parties passed in and out of the church, and all the normal functions of the parish continued undisturbed, after the first wild rush for food was over. The guilds and societies maintained their work among the sick and the poor, and the church was open from six in the morning until six in the evening. Each of its rectors in turn has sought to meet all needs with practical kindness, to feed the hungry, shrive the sinner and succour the unfortunate.

Except for one brief flurry in December, 1921, when two vestrymen and two priests resigned, Transfiguration has never been touched by the breath of controversy. Dr. Houghton was in the south for his health at the time and was much disturbed that a rift should have developed during his absence. Even when ecclesiastical dissension has raged all around it, the church has been amazingly free from agitation, sailing unruffled on the blue waters of tolerance. Presbyterians, Baptists and Methodists have been married before its Eucharistic Lights, and the strictest nonconformist has accepted its highly developed æsthetic ritual as a matter of course. Dr. Ray admits that he is the first of the three rectors to raise his voice in a partisan discussion, except for the founder's avowed stand on abolition. In February, 1930, he took a definite stand against prohibition:

> From this historic pulpit that ever has lifted its voice in the interest of humanity, I plead for some remedial legislation which will replace our present lawless era. I feel I must risk partisanship, a thing the church has never had in its history, for this is a crusade and something must be done to save New York and the country from the effects of prohibition. I unhesitatingly assert that from my own experience in a parish that is known the world over for its philanthropy and humanitarian work, where the doors are open at all hours to the needs of all classes, I find the rapid increase of drinking among our boys and girls under sixteen years of age, the number of girls in our rescue homes and the increase of deaths from alcoholism, not only among the rich but in every class, to be simply appalling. We want honesty, temperance and sobriety instead of blatant corruption and hypocrisy.

Dr. Ray's liberality has been exemplified in the various uses to which he has lent the church. One of the most picturesque wedding parties that ever passed through the lich-gate was a cinema group being filmed for *The Street of Forgotten Men*. The "bride" was Mary Brian and she was followed by a group of bridesmaids. Percy Marmont stood outside the

imp RLB   RLBoyer

THE LICH GATE Looking EAST

lich-gate as a beggar with his tin cup. He was so realistic in the rôle that he had difficulty in keeping people from dropping coppers in his cup. Jack Dempsey and Estelle Taylor also used The Little Church Around the Corner for one of their pictures. It has been reproduced repeatedly in stage settings and the wedding party in the finale of *Sally* stood before the lich-gate with the actors' church in the background. In the spring of 1929 Dean Cornwell, commissioned to paint the history of California in twelve great panels for the new library in Los Angeles, returned from the largest studio he could find abroad—Sargent's in London—and was granted the use of the Guild Hall by Dr. Ray to pose the Bishop who moves through the historical scenes of his murals. Mr. Cornwell needed ecclesiastical vestments, the dalmatic, cope, mitre and other properties of the church. Theatrical costumers had none of the required articles. So the model came to the Guild Hall and attired himself in the necessary vestments.

On the Sunday following Easter, 1930, Dr. Ray announced the foundation of The Family of The Little Church Around the Corner, the first alumni association of any church in the world. He explained that his plan was to link together the million persons who have had contact of one sort or another with the parish. The visitors' book shows that they are scattered around the globe—in Trinidad, England, Abyssinia, Germany, Scotland, China, Japan, Ireland, the Hawaiian Islands, Canada, South America, France, Spain and Russia, as well as in every State of the Union. Their letters testify to the affection in which they hold the church. Dr. Ray pointed out from the pulpit that, while an endowment fund was necessary to carry on the work, the larger object was to crystallize sentiment in order to keep the church where it is, safe from the destroying forces of a growing city.

To-day the little church of 1848 has grown into a gracious mother of beauty, numbering her children by the hundreds of thousands. There is no more beloved parish in all the world and I, her third rector, completing the first mystical cycle of my rectorate, to-day am celebrating my seventh anniversary and entering my sabbatical year. I, too, have seen a vision and dreamed a dream.

I see the fair future of greater usefulness and a more complete life for the church which truly is a house of prayer for all people. It is a national shrine serving all men everywhere. It must be preserved through the years to come. How can that be done in New York, where no building is safe, where all must be levelled to the ground to make way for progress, for rampant and prosperous commercialism?

Already towering business buildings surround the church and jostle rudely its garden walls. Money alone will not do it. There is one thing, however, that is greater than big business, more powerful than millions of dollars. It is human sentiment. This church is hallowed by it. To-day I am announcing the organization of this sentiment for the purpose of saving the church as a national shrine for generations to come, as a medium of God's love to men. This organization is to be called The Family of The Little Church Around the Corner.

The history of the church has been inseparable from the old site where the founder created a tradition of his own. For eighty years the parish has maintained its individuality and a storm of protest greeted the suggestion put forward at one time that it should follow the tide uptown. It was felt that no modern temple of stone or marble could replace the cloistered charm of the original edifice in its shady garden setting. Thus, while skyscraper churches match their spires against the towers of commerce, the Church of the Transfiguration clings to its quiet acre, a romantic shrine in an empyrean city, protected by a family scattered to the far corners of the earth.

INDEX

INDEX

INDEX

INDEX

Hoffman, Governor, 60

Holland, Edward, 42

Holland, E. M., 123

Holland, George, Jefferson called merriest actor, 41; funeral, 44; desk in Guild Hall, 122

Holland, Joseph William, married, 144

Holland, Kate, 123

Holland, Mrs. Catherine, 69

Hopper, De Wolf, 77

Houghton, Anna, 24, 113

Houghton, Mary Gertrude (Mrs. Charles Strombom), daughter of second rector, 76; married Rev. Charles Strombom, 82; death and burial of, 134; memorial window installed to her father, Rev. George Clarke Houghton, D.D., 118; memorial window of, 134

Houghton, Mrs. George Clarke (Mary Creemer Pirsson), Lady Chapel as memorial, 2, 81; married Rev. George Clarke Houghton, D.D., 76; death of, 81; Rood Wall memorial to, 117

Houghton, Mrs. George Hendric (Caroline Graves Anthon), marriage to Rev. George Hendric Houghton, 24; relative of Mrs. Stuyvesant Fish, 57

Houghton, Rev. Edward C., 69

Houghton, Rev. George Clarke, D.D., second rector, 2; during rectorate church became the marrying church, 2; built Lady Chapel as memorial to his wife, 4, 81; vicar in 1897, 75; curate at Trinity, 75; rector of Trinity, Hoboken, 76; married Mary Creemer Pirsson, 76; founded *The Kalendar*, 79; death of his wife, 81; puts ban on hasty marriages, 84; Golden Jubilee, 101; death and burial, 104; Rood Wall memorial to his wife, 117; windows of the Beatitudes as memorial to his uncle, the first rector, 117; altar in Chapel of the Holy Family memorial to, 141

Houghton, Rev. George Hendric, D.D., founder and first rector of Transfiguration, 2; came to New York, 10; parent-age, 10; graduated from University of City of New York, 12; studied theology, 13; ordained, 14; broached subject of parish for the poor, 15; began parish in Dr. Lawson Carter's home, 15; naming of parish, 17; notice of completion of church, 19; in the squalor of the Five Points, 20; taught Hebrew in General Theological Seminary, 23; married Caroline Graves Anthon, 24; promoting Anglo-Catholic revival, 28; leadership in High Church ritual, 30; abolitionist, 31; with refugees during riots, 31; Holland's funeral, 44; popular with acting profession, 44; funds to Chicago fire sufferers, 46; favorite with boys and girls, 60; daily Eucharist, 1880, 63; fondest wish—the Lich-Gate, 69; death and funeral, 71; windows of the Beatitudes memorial to, 117

Howard, Mrs. Carrington, 143

Howland, A. R., 117

Howland, Georgiana, 117

Howland, Rev. Dr. Robert S., 117

Hoyt, Eugenia Bankhead, 146

Hoyt, Morton H., 146

Huggins, Miller, funeral, 131

Hughson, Rev. Shirley Carter, 102

Hull, Mrs. Shelley, 124

Huntington, Rev. W. R., 65

Hurry, Mrs. Emily B., 62

Irving, Henry, 66

Irwin, Will, 93

Janauschek, Fanny, 123

Jefferson, Joseph, gave popular name, 1, 9; memorial to, 132; in *Rip Van Winkle*, 40; plans Holland's funeral, 41; phrase, "God bless the little church around the corner," 43; regular attendant, 47; on records as godfather, 48; song dedicated to, 51; death of, 78; poem, "Immortality," 131; unveiling of memorial to, 131; description of memorial, 132

Jessay, Julieenia, married, 144

Jordan, George Edwin, married, 146

INDEX

INDEX

memory of William Walter Griffin, 96; tablet in memory of William Judson Minor, 100; window to honour actors and actresses, 133; windows in memory of Ann Aurora Ballow, 116; David Loney Bruce-Brown, 117; Edwin Booth, 78; John Drew, 132; Mrs. George Clarke Houghton, 25, 117; Rev. George Clarke Houghton, D.D., 118; Rev. George Hendric Houghton, D.D., 117; Joseph Jefferson, 132; Harry Montague, 47; José Maria Munoz, 118; Clarence Pell, 118; Mary Shaw, 133; Mrs. Charles Strombom, 134; Mrs. Richard S. Willis, 22;

Miller, Henry, 123, 130

Mills, Grace A., 111

Miniature of Crucifixion, gift of Mme. de Verdi, 117

Minor, William Judson, 100

Mitchell, Grant, 121

Moller, Adelina S., 95

Montague, Harry, communicant, 3; buried from, 47; memorial, 47; at the height of his power, 120

Moore, Clement C., 8

Moore, George Henry, 13

Moore, Percy, 122

Morris, Clara, funeral of, 127–128; in *L'Article* 47, *Camille* and *East Lynne*, 128

Morris, Daniel H., married, 146

Motto of parish, *Fides opera*, 20

Mowe, Mrs. William Robert, 101, 115

Mowe, Robert W., 104

Muhlenberg, Rev. William A., 13

Mulle, Ida, 124

Munoz, José Maria, memorial, 118

Murray, Robert, 9

Newman, Cardinal, 29

O'Brien, Colonel H. J., 32

Order of the Holy Cross, 63

Organ, modern, installed, 69

Organ, new, 117

Outcault, Mary Jane, married, 145

Page, Walter Hines, 93

Parish House, gift of, by Mrs. Sarah J. Zabriskie, 68

Parkhurst, Rev. Charles H., D.D., 37, 73

Pease, Rev. Lewis Morris, 20

Peck, Mary Francis, memorial, 118

Peck, Mrs. Thomas Bloodgood, 118

Peck, Thomas Bloodgood, 118

Pell, Clarence, memorial window, 118

Pershing, Frank Edwin, married, 145

Pickford, Mary, 143

Pirsson, Mary Creemer, 76

Pirsson, Talbot, 76

Play, *The Little Church Around the Corner*, 50

Players, The, 67, 78

Pollock, Mrs. Channing, 124

Poor Player at the Gate, The, poem, 52

Potter, Rev. Henry Codman, 39, 72, 85

Potter, Rt. Rev. Horatio, 24, 29

Prime, William C., 117

Pulpit, memorial to Rev. William and Mrs. Staunton, 118

Quintard, Edward A., 34

Rainsford, Rev. William S., 73

Rappelyea, James, 100

Ray, Mrs. Jackson H., 112

Ray, Mrs. Jackson H. Randolph (Mary Elmendorf Watson) married Rev. Jackson H. Randolph Ray, D.D., 110

Ray, Kathryna, 133

Ray, Rev. Jackson H. Randolph, D.D., third rector, 3; presented to parish by second rector, 103; announced as rector, 105; education, 107; newspaper experience, 108; ordination, 108; in Texas, 109; marriage to Mary Elmendorf Watson, 110; founded Actors Guild, 121; dinner in honor of, 125; consulted Evangeline Adams, 146; bread line, 152; founded alumni, The Family of the Little Church Around the Corner, 155

Raymond, Mrs. Charles H., 143

INDEX

INDEX

Taft, Marcus Lorenzo, 13
Talmage, Rev. T. De Witt, D.D., 37, 64
Taylor, Estelle, 155
Terry, Ellen, 124
Thomas, Frederick C., married, 92
Thompson, Lysander, 44
Tower, Mrs. Charles H., 122
Transfiguration, choice of name, 17; window, 94–95
Tyng, Rev. Stephen H., D.D., 12, 65
Tyng, Rev. Stephen H., Jr., D.D., 39

Underground Station, Church of Transfiguration sheltered Negro refugees, 31

Van Brunt, Jessie, 133
Van Cleve, Florence, writer of poem, *The Little Church Around the Corner*, 53
Vandenhoff, George, 51
Verdi, Mme. de, 117

Wallack, Arthur, married, 144
Wallack, James W., 48, 130

Wallack, Lester, 3, 44, 144
Wambold, D. S., writer of music for *God Bless the Little Church Around the Corner*, 49; song used at unveiling of Jefferson memorial, 131, married, 144
Warfield, David, 128
Watson, Mary Elmendorf, 110
Weaver, David, 144
Welles, Alice, 101
Whiffen, Mrs. Thomas, 78, 123
White, Grace Norma, married, 144
White, Richard, 58
White, Stanford, 58, 78
Wickland, Lyons, first bridegroom in Chapel of the Holy Family, 142
Willis, Mrs. Richard S., memorial, 22
Wilson, Elizabeth, memorial, 35
Wilson, George, doorkeeper, 31, 35
Wilson, Walter, funeral, 131
Wise, Tom, funeral, 131

Zabriskie, Mrs. Sarah J., 68, 116
Zogbaum, Harry St. Clair, married, 143